TYNEHAM

THE LOST VILLAGE OF DORSET

TYNEHAM

THE LOST VILLAGE OF DORSET

ANDREW NORMAN AND MARY HURST

HALSGROVE

First published in Great Britain in 2003
Reprinted 2005
Copyright © 2003 Andrew Norman

Front Cover: *'The Street', Tyneham, painted in watercolour by John Grant.*

British Library Cataloguing-in-Publication Data
A CIP record for this title is available from the British Library

ISBN 1 84114 322 7

HALSGROVE

Halsgrove House
Lower Moor Way
Tiverton, Devon EX16 6SS
Tel: 01884 243242
Fax: 01884 243325
email: sales@halsgrove.com
website: www.halsgrove.com

Printed and bound by
The Cromwell Press, Trowbridge

CONTENTS

ABOUT THE AUTHORS

Andrew Norman was born in Newbury and educated at Thornhill High School, Gwelo, Southern Rhodesia (now Zimbabwe) and at St Edmund Hall, Oxford, where he read animal physiology. In December 1970 he graduated in medicine from the Radcliffe Infirmary and went into general practice in Poole, Dorset. In 1983 he sustained a back injury which forced him to give up his career: he is now a full-time writer.

Mary Hurst was born in Bournemouth and has been a writer for some time. She became a nurse at St Bartholomew's Hospital, London, before taking a sideways step into medical Social Work. She then married a Royal Navy pilot and lived in the Far East. Her prize-winning dissertation on cancer care has been used as a basis for setting up a Hospice Service abroad. Mary returned to Bournemouth in 1986 with her two sons and daughter and took up nursing again. Andrew and Mary met in 1991 and they have collaborated on various literary projects.

Also by Andrew Norman:
HMS Hood: *Pride of the Royal Navy*
By Swords Divided
T.E. Lawrence, Unravelling the Enigma

This book is a tribute to all those people whose village of
Tyneham was sacrificed for the sake of their country.
We hope that through Helen Taylor's memories it will remain
a true and living record of their voices.

ACKNOWLEDGEMENTS

We are indebted to many former residents of the parish of Tyneham-cum-Steeple for the sharing of the reminiscences, the loan of photographs and for all the help and encouragement, particularly to General H.M.G. Bond, the late Helen Taylor, the late Margot Bond, George and Sylvia Braisby, Joseph Dando, Kathleen Barnes, Mabel Taylor and Arthur Grant. Also to Joan Brachi, Jenny Elmes, Winnie Applin, George Willey, Nancy Henshaw, Meg Ritchie, Brigid Chapman, John Mayes, David Haysom, Julie Astin and Cyril Barnes.

Our thanks to Jean Norman for checking the proofs; Linda Price of Durlston Country Park Information Centre, Swanage; the Dorset County Museum; Dorset County Archivist and Tony Ellis (Archivist) and Angela Fisher (Assistant Archivist) of the Maritime Coastguard Agency at bridlington. Also to Brian Wead of the RNLI Poole and to the staff of Poole Library and the Reference Library; to *Country Life* magazine for permission to reproduce the photograph of the Chintz Bedroom; to Dovecote Press for permission to use Lillian Bond's book *Tyneham, A Lost Heritage*; and to the Dorset Archives Service for permission to reproduce an entry from the Tyneham Marriage Register of 1943 and particularly to Range Liaison Officer Mick Burgess of Lulworth Range Control and Range Controller and staff at the Photographic Section, Royal Armoured Corps, Bovington, for supplying archive material and for permission to use official photographs.

PREFACE

The significance of Tyneham – a tiny village near the south coast of England in Dorset – lies in its remoteness, screened as it is by great hills on three sides, with the sea on the fourth. It therefore remained, through much of the twentieth century, in a kind of time capsule (representative of life in a bygone, never-to-be-repeated age) until its peace was finally shattered for ever in November, 1943 following the advent of the Second World War. It was at this time that the Army requisitioned the parish – including the village – for a gunnery range.

Our interest in Tyneham arose from the fact that one of its residents – Miss Helen Taylor, one-time seamstress at Tyneham House – spent her final years in a nursing home owned by me, Dr Andrew Norman, when she was in her nineties. We were able to hear at first hand, what life was really like in a place where labour and laughter lived side by side. Tyneham even had a language of its own and yes, there was even the occasional romance!

Our research led us down a myriad of exciting avenues. We tracked down and interviewed several former residents who relived their memories and generously provided us with photographs, and General Mark Bond, son of Ralph, the last owner of Tyneham was able to give us his perspective, as a member of the family who had owned the house and estate for generations.

We invite the reader to make a journey back in time, with Miss Taylor, who brings the village and its people – from parlour-maid to parson, and from schoolteacher to squire – back to life!

INTRODUCTION

Helen Taylor looked up from the armchair in which she was sitting and smiled. 'Oh yes,' she said with feeling, 'Tyneham was a very special place. I could tell you some lovely tales about Tyneham and the people who lived there.'

And then she began to talk: not about a lost village or ruined cottages for everyone knows that Tyneham is no more, but about Tyneham as she knew it, a living, vibrant community. This little Dorset village, 2 miles east of Lulworth Cove, had existed for centuries, nestling isolated and undisturbed in a sheltered corner of a beautiful county. Rural life had continued, uninterrupted by the turmoil of the world beyond. And then suddenly, on a bleak winter's night just before the Christmas of 1943, the lives of the inhabitants of the parish of Tyneham-cum-Steeple were changed for ever – their fate sealed by the stroke of a pen wielded in the War Office, Whitehall. The area was to be requisitioned for military use and the villagers, many of them elderly, were to be evacuated and billeted throughout the Isle of Purbeck. This, they were told, was to be their contribution to the war effort, and they were given verbal assurances that when hostilities ceased, they would be permitted to return to their homes.

In the event, this did not happen. The inhabitants were never to return. This is their story, seen through the eyes of Helen Taylor, formerly a seamstress at Tyneham House. Her memories of the village and the people who lived there give an insight into an aspect of life in rural Dorset that has disappeared for ever.

Helen Taylor was forty-two when she left Tyneham in December 1943, along with 250 other villagers who had given up their homes for their country. She was the last resident to leave, but before going and with a heavy heart, she wrote these words which were pinned to the door of St Mary's church:

Please treat the church and houses with care. We have given up our homes where many of us lived for generations to help win the war to keep men free. We shall return one day and thank you for treating the village kindly.

Although she understood the needs of the Army and never showed any resentment, she often felt sad at the loss of a close-knit community which spanned generations.

Helen Taylor returned in 1998 when, at the age of ninety-seven, she was laid to rest beside her mother and her elder sister in the family plot in St Mary's churchyard. At long last she would be at peace in the place she loved most – Tyneham, her home.

Helen Taylor in 1988: the garden seat is said to be made from barrel staves of smuggled brandy casks!

1
VOICES FROM THE PAST

The air is as fresh today upon my face as it was when I was a young girl all those years ago, and as I look down on the village of Tyneham, memories come flooding back. It has been a long and arduous climb for me, at the age of seventy-three, across great earthen ramparts and ditches to the top of this hill for I am standing on Flowers Barrow, an Iron Age fort on Dorset's south coast. It is surrounded by the most beautiful scenery you could ever wish to see. There is not another soul in sight, at least not another living person. There are plenty of sheep, rooks and seagulls, deer, badgers and the occasional bird of prey. But it is easy to imagine other souls, caught in a different dimension, who are here in spirit, held by the magnetism of this special place. I can almost hear their voices mingling with the gentle breeze brushing my cheeks – my old friends, so many of them long gone, and voices from even further back in time…

Flowers Barrow, which is a fort rather than an ancient grave-mound, covers 15 acres of ground and stands 600ft above sea level. It was once twice that size, but the sea has nibbled away at the cliffs, and over the centuries has brought half of them crashing down onto the beach. It is believed that it is named after a Roman officer called Florus but long before his legions marched across this lush countryside, others lived and breathed the pure air. Many of the late Bronze and early Iron Age hilltop barrows still house a skeleton buried in a crouched position, curled up like a foetus, a drinking-cup placed at the head so that the soul has food and drink to sustain it on its journey beyond this earthly life.

There are 20 of these burial chambers on nearby Povington Hill alone, the largest one measuring 56ft (60m) in diameter and 7ft (1.80m) in height, built for the local chieftain and his family. On the slopes of nearby Gold Down and Whiteway Hill, the rectangular outlines of later Celtic fields are still clearly visible.

Near this place have been found amulets made out of the soft, friable Kimmeridge shale-stone and polished to a shiny black lustre. These lucky charms to ward off the evil eye were worn as bracelets or as part of a necklace and made by the Celtic tribe, *Dwr y Triges* – 'the people near the tidal water' – who gave their name to the county. The Romans, who

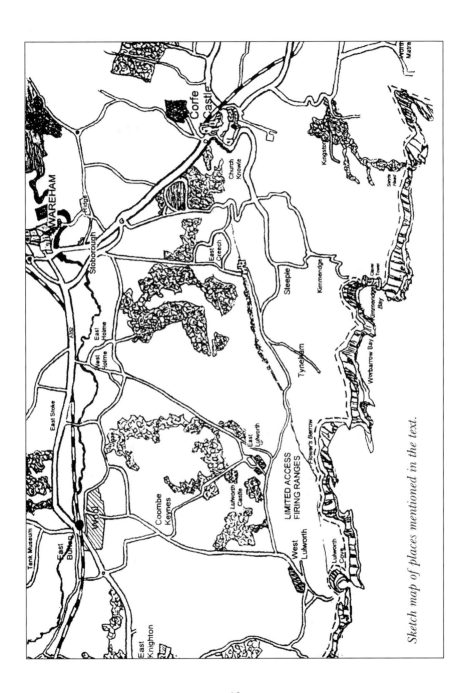

Sketch map of places mentioned in the text.

13

called them Durotriges, so admired the amulets that they continued to produce them after their invasion in the first century AD. According to the eighteenth-century Dorset historian, the Revd John Hutchins, there were two manufactuaries near here, one at Povington and another at Kimmeridge. The Roman women wore these good-luck charms even to the grave, as a tomb excavation in Dorchester has revealed.

There is more that brings me, elderly and alone, to such a remote place as this. I come not simply because of my fascination for the ancient past, or because of the breathtaking views of the sea and the cliffs to the south, or the vast expanse of heath and farmland which rolls northwards towards Corfe Castle, Wareham and the silvery waters of Poole Harbour which are visible to the northeast.

No, it is the more recent past which compels me. When I made myself the promise that I would come back I was told it was a mistake to return to a place where you have once lived, but I could not resist it. I had to make one last visit to the area which was my entire world for forty-one years – a world whose limits I can see before me now, and beyond whose limits I never ventured nor felt the need to. Below me I can see Tyneham Church, the school, the one-and-only street with its line of houses which we used to call The Row, and my beloved Laundry Cottage where our family lived. Along the path that leads down the seashore and Worbarrow Bay are the fishermen's cottages and the old lifeboat station. Up the valley, or 'gwyle' as we call it, and through the trees I can glimpse part of Tyneham House. But it is not as it used to be.

No longer do I hear the shouts of happy children, the clip-clop of horses' hooves, the voices of men harvesting the fields, or the cries of the auctioneer on the beach selling off the catch of fish. All is quiet and the buildings I describe now lie in ruin, and the life I once knew, and the community of which I was once a part, is no more.

2
NO SMALL SACRIFICE...

It was on 17 November 1943 that the news broke – I remember it as if it were yesterday. Everyone in the village was rushing round asking each other, 'Have you had yours yet?' They were referring to the letters from Southern Command which had been delivered to each household by Charlie Beauchamp, the postmaster at nearby Creech village.

My sister, Bessie, was hanging out the washing at Laundry Cottage where we lived when we received our letter. She had just finished a load for the big house and was taking advantage of a fine day and a drying easterly wind to get it aired and I was giving her a hand. Charlie knew the contents before we opened it because all the letters bore the same tidings and when he handed me ours, I noticed he had a tear in his eye. As I opened the envelope and began to read the contents out loud, Bessie came and sat down on the stool beside me. The letter, which was signed 'C H Miller, Major-General i/c Administration, Southern Command, began:

In order to give our troops the fullest opportunity to perfect their training in the use of modern weapons of war, the Army must have an area of land particularly suited to their special needs and in which they can use live shells. For this reason you will realise the chosen area must be cleared of all civilians.

It went on:

... The most careful search has been made to find an area suitable for the Army's purpose and which, at the same time, will involve the smallest number of persons and property. The area decided on, after the most careful consultation between the Government authorities concerned, lies roughly inside the square formed by East Lulworth – East Stoke – East Holme – Kimmeridge Bay.

Here, in handwriting, someone had written: 'Including your properties – see overleaf.'
I continued to read:

It is regretted that, in the National Interest, it is necessary to move you from your homes, and everything possible will be done to help you, both by payment of compensation, and by finding other accommodation for you if you are unable to do so yourself.

The date on which the Military will take over this area is the 19th December next, and all civilians must be out of the area by that date.

A special office will be opened at Westport House, WAREHAM, on Wednesday the 17th November, and you will be able to get advice between the hours of 10am and 7pm from there on your personal problems and difficulties. Any letters should be sent to that address also for the present.

The Government appreciate that this is no small sacrifice which you are asked to make, but they are sure that you will give this further help towards winning the war with a good heart.

Bessie and I looked at each other blankly. The area was already an armed camp with barbed wire and tank obstacles erected along the beach, and soldiers on patrol both day and night. Since the outbreak of war on 3 September 1939, Mr Ralph Bond of Tyneham House had organised the Home Guard into an efficient fighting force with himself in command of the Tyneham, Kimmeridge and Steeple platoon. He had previous experience of two years in the Officer Training Corps at Eton and was very keen on target practice. 'Come on,' he would say to his troops on a Sunday afternoon, 'We shall go down to the gravel pit and pop off a few rounds.'

The Royal Air Force, which had established a radar station at Brandy Bay near the cliffs at Tyneham Cap, had requisitioned Tyneham House to accommodate members of the Women's Auxiliary Air Force from that station, which had proved most effective when an incursion by German E boats was foiled earlier in the year. The airmen were billeted at the rectory and William Bond and his wife, Evelyn, had therefore to move out and into Museum Cottage – so called because this was where their children had once kept natural history specimens. However, while their new abode was being made ready for them, the Bonds spent a short time with us at Laundry Cottage.

Had it really come to this? Did we really have to leave our homes? And if so where were we to go? Some of us had been to the village of Corfe 5 miles away, or even as far as the market town of Wareham on the River Frome, but many had not even ventured as far as that. This was our life, here in the valley, the only life we knew and as far as we were concerned, there was no other.

I looked at the letter again. And there, below the message, was the name of our home 'Laundry Cottage, Tyneham' and the names of the holders of the tenancy, namely my sister and myself – 'B. and H. Taylor' – Bessie and Helen.

It appeared that the whole of the Tyneham Valley including Worbarrow, Tyneham village and house, Baltington, North and South Egliston and Lutton, was to be evacuated.

The Possession Order did not refer to the village of Steeple or to a large area north of Whiteway Hill including Povington and West Creech with all the farms and smallholdings. A total of 225 people would have to leave their homes, 40 from Tyneham Village and the remaining 185 from the north side of the hill. My heart breaking, I turned to Bessie and said:

'So that is that, I suppose.'

She nodded sadly. We loved Tyneham but we also loved our country and if it was our duty to leave for the war effort, then so be it. Nevertheless we were both left in a state of shock, yet we tried to hide our fear and the hurt which lay deep inside us.

3
BEGINNINGS

When I refer to Tyneham as 'My Tyneham', that is of course only a figure of speech. All the land was owned by the Bond family, of which there are several branches throughout the Isle of Purbeck, and all our dwellings were rented from them.

The Bonds came originally from Cornwall. Denis Bond was one of the Commissioners who were engaged in the trial of King Charles I; Thomas Bond was Comptroller of the household of Queen Henrietta Maria, the mother of Charles II and was instrumental in the building of Bond Street in London. John Bond, born in 1555, was a merchant who travelled widely and was not averse to a little privateering when it suited him. Lady Alice Lisle, granddaughter of William Bond of Blackmanstone here in Purbeck, was sentenced to death by Judge Jeffreys for harbouring a refugee from the Battle of Sedgemoor. She was beheaded at Winchester on 2 September 1685, after the judge was persuaded by public outcry and indignation to alter his original sentence of 'death by burning'.

Mr William Henry Bond, or Mr W.H. Bond as he preferred to be called rather than Squire which would have been his title in former times, was a fine upstanding man in his mid-sixties who had served as a lieutenant in the Royal Scots. He had inherited the estate in 1898 on the death of his uncle the Reverend John Bond.

Mr W.H. Bond saw himself and his family as custodians of Tyneham and he felt it his duty to ensure that the estate was kept in good order for the generations to come. In plain language he expected people to keep the place tidy and anyone who failed to do so was told off. He had a particular aversion to thistles and was often to be seen prowling around with his hoe ready to deal summarily with any he might find. Despite his forthright manner, however, the villagers regarded him as a father figure to whom they could always turn in time of need.

He was a creature of routine and was always pleased early in the morning to see his newspaper, freshly ironed by the butler, ready for him on the table in the Oak Hall. Newspapers were delivered to Creech village on the north side of the hill with the afternoon post and had to

The arms of Bond of Tyneham and Moigne Combe.
Photo Martin Bond

William Taylor, my father.
Photo: Helen Taylor

Emily Taylor, my mother.
Photo: Helen Taylor

be collected from there. This meant, much to his disappointment, that he was always a day late with the news. In former times he took the *Western Gazette* which the baker brought with him from Stoborough, near Corfe Castle, but now he took *The Globe*.

My family came here in 1902, the year after the old Queen had died and had been succeeded by our new King Edward VII. My father, William, was working for the Kindersley family of Clyffe House, Tincleton near Dorchester, when he saw an advertisement for a woodman to work on the Tyneham estate. Father discussed it with my mother, Emily, whose dream it had always been to live by the sea and when he duly applied and was appointed she was delighted. I was then a mere babe-in-arms and our family included Arthur and Bert Taylor, my older brothers; Bessie, my sister; and William and Charlie Meech, my mother's sons by her first marriage.

Why did Tyneham come to mean so much to me? Was it because of its charming buildings, its animals, its remoteness, the naturalness of its surroundings, its proximity to the sea which was a great novelty to all of us? Yes, of course these were factors, but mainly it was the people, the wonderful characters whom we grew to know and love, whether lowly like Willie Mintern the smallholder's son – alas, he did not live to make old bones but died in an accident at sea – or exalted like the Bonds whom we counted as our friends despite the difference in station.

No one could afford to be idle so when we moved into our new home my mother, Emily, became the laundress for Tyneham House and the rectory. Our home, which was aptly named Laundry Cottage, was therefore for her also a place of work. It had the distinction of being the only dwelling in the village to have running water, which was just as well or we could never have managed. Everyone else had to fetch their water in buckets from the village pump.

The laundry arrived every Monday morning and was delivered in two huge wicker hampers by my stepbrother, Charlie Meech, in his cart, for he was the odd-job man or 'odd man' as we called him. Laundry Cottage was actually two semi-detached buildings and so it could accommodate our extended family. In the yard at the back of the house was a copper – a huge metal cauldron which could hold 40 gallons of water. It was set in a brick surround with a stone step which was just as well or mother, who was not very tall, would have been unable to reach into it.

Underneath the copper was a fire of wooden faggots, bundles of which were provided for the purpose. After boiling, and being stirred around in the soapy water with a wooden paddle, the laundry was rinsed in two big wooden troughs, or 'trows' as we called them, and then passed through a wringer with rubber rollers before being hung out on the line to dry.

There was a ledge around the coke stove on which my mother, when she was doing the ironing, could stand the irons to keep them hot. She was strong, sturdy and most particular about hygiene, for we had all heard about the terrible epidemic of cholera at Dorchester. This had occurred when prisoners brought down from London were housed in the town's empty cavalry barracks. Their infected clothes and bedding had contaminated the water supply.

Every month my mother, along with the other village women including the rector's wife, walked the 5 miles to Wareham to stock up with provisions. These they loaded onto perambulators which they had taken with them for the purpose. Mother was in demand not only for her prowess as a laundress. As the nearest doctor was several hours ride away, she was often consulted owing to her expertise in the use of plants and herbs for medicinal purposes. All agreed that her nettle-and-dandelion tea was an excellent restorative and for burns, spiders' cobwebs were found to be efficacious. Mother was always informed if someone was 'expecting', and would attend the birth whether by day or by night. She was also caretaker for the church and school.

People used to say my father, William, was a solitary man and it was true. There was nothing he liked better than to be out in the woods communing with nature and listening to the melodic sound of the birds, rather than having to endure what he perceived as the endless banter and babblings of human beings. His tasks included the collecting and bundling up of sticks for the fires, cutting the branches of sweet chestnuts for hurdles, or coppicing hazel to make the spars which held the thatch in place when a roof was being remade. Or he might find himself logging in Tyneham Great Wood, Rookery Wood, or Limekiln Plantation and then stacking the timber to season for the sawmill, the carpenter or the boat-builder. Floorboards, milking-stools, handles for spades or pitchforks, chairs, tables and carts – so many things were made out of wood in those days. And, of course, the bark of the trees could always be sold and used in the tanning of leather. There was always another hedge to be layered or fence to be mended.

Disposing of the ancient elm tree, 1910, prior to planting 'Coronation oak'.
Photo: Crown copyright

The cattle must be kept in and deer kept out. It is amazing what damage deer can do to young trees newly planted.

Father's biggest challenge was in 1911 when the old elm tree which stood at the top of The Row just outside the churchyard was found to be rotten. It was considered to be a danger to passers-by and had to be chopped down and disposed of. Every able-bodied man in the village turned out to lend a hand and the task took several days.

It was decided to replace the tree with an oak to commemorate the coronation of King George V, which had taken place the year before. Miss Margot Bond, daughter of Mr W.H. Bond, kindly agreed to plant it, even though she was in mourning for the death in India of her brother Algernon.

The whole village turned out and everyone applauded the planting of our Coronation Oak. Mr Bond invited us to drink the health of King

George, Queen Mary and the Royal Family. He supplied beer for the men and the women and we children were given mineral water which I did not think very much of, if I can say this without sounding ungrateful! The ceremony ended with us all singing the National Anthem after which Mr Bond gave packets of tobacco to the men and tea to the women. We children received sweets and bananas. Three cheers were given for Mr and Mrs Bond and for the rector, the Reverend Claude Homan, and his wife.

'May our new King live for ever' we all said.

4
WILLINGLY TO SCHOOL

The school was within a stone's throw of our house and I was so keen to learn that even before the age of five I would join the others in the playground and try to sneak into the classroom without the teacher noticing – but she always did. I was particularly envious of my older sister, Bessie, who had started school a full two years earlier. Finally I was enrolled as a pupil; it was the happiest day of my life so far.

The school was established in the year 1860 by the Reverend Nathaniel Bond of Grange, a village to the north on the other side of the hill. He was a distant relative of the Bond's of Tyneham and built the school at his own expense, using materials left over from the demolition of an old tithe barn. It consisted of one large room, with a raised platform at the far end screened by a curtain where the infants had their desks. One drawback however, was the absence of any windows on the south wall which meant we had to rely on candles to light the

The schoolroom, with Union flag which children saluted every morning.

classroom for a large part of the year. It also meant that even in spring and autumn it was often so cold that the 'tortoise' stove had to be kept burning. In wet weather the stove's large fireguard was used for hanging the children's soggy clothes and boots on, and in the meantime they would be provided temporarily with clothes and slippers purchased out of school funds.

The school's head teacher was Miss Norah Woodman and she lived in the northernmost cottage of The Row. Between it and the school was the school yard with a gate across to keep out the farm animals. Her niece, Miss Gladys Wright, was in charge of the infants. She taught us to count with beads, and we drew pictures with coloured crayons of the wonderful variety of flowers and ferns we collected on our nature walks. When the dentist came to the school it was here in the schoolroom that he set up his pedal-driven drill, and that is the only time I regretted having to attend.

Above the fireplace hung a large portrait of our late-lamented King Edward VII – 'The old king with the beard' as we called him. Also on display were two lines which I had composed myself and written out in my best handwriting:

Lost – several golden moments between sunrise and sunset.
No reward is offered, as they are gone forever.

Everyone had to pay to go to school – 2d per child per month, or 3d per family. This amount was not sufficient to pay Miss Woodman's salary of £25 a year and her assistant, Miss Wright's, salary of £4 a year, together with the cost of fuel, light and books, so it had to be supplemented by voluntary contributions.

At nine o'clock all the children assembled in the playground in a long line waiting for rector, the Reverend Claude Homan, who had married Mary, a member of the Digby family from Studland Manor on the east Dorset coast. The biggest boy or girl was chosen to stand by the front door with the Union Jack as everybody marched round the playground and around the flag, saluting it in turn. There followed hymns and prayers and a scripture lesson taken by the rector, who would then be available to lend a hand should any extra help with teaching be required.

We children took cocoa powder and sugar to school; it was mixed with water and heated up on the stove at break-time and we drank it from

Helen Taylor with dog, Spot. Photo: Helen Taylor

The Class of 1912 in their 'Sunday Best'.   Photo: Julie Astin

our enamel mugs. At midday the ceremony of saluting the flag was repeated and the local children went home for lunch. Those from farther afield ate the sandwiches which they had brought. There was no homework as everything was done in the classroom. Miss Wright was strict and not averse to rapping a boy or girl across the knuckles if he or she failed to hold a pen correctly or do the joined-up writing which she insisted upon from the start. However she had our best interests at heart and used to buy with money from her own pocket potatoes and the ingredients for soup, rather than see any of us go hungry.

Although the main core of pupils continued their education right through until they reached the age of fourteen, others came and went when, for example, a parent might hear of a farmer in another area offering an extra shilling or two in wages. Those fortunate enough to be employed at Tyneham House however, could generally be sure of having a job for life. Absenteeism was sometimes a problem but this was due largely to the great distances pupils were obliged to walk to school – one mile for those from the village of Lutton and 2 miles for those from Steeple Leaze. In summer time this was not a problem but in winter when snow or mud lay on the ground and gales and blizzards cut like a knife, then it was a different matter. Miss Woodman often sent despairing letters to the Attendance Officer but in the circumstances there was little that could be done.

Illness was another reason for absence from school. Bessie and I were kept at home when our brother, Bert, caught diphtheria, which he fortunately survived, thanks largely to mother's skilful ministrations. Nurse Jones excluded Judy, Maggie and Daisy Warr for having 'verminous heads' and Dr Drury advised Evelyn Longman, when she had impetigo, to stay at home until the scabs had cleared. When Maggie Warr had a discharging ear, Mrs Mary Bond of Tyneham House paid for her to convalesce for three weeks by the sea at Swanage as it was thought the change of air would do her good.

Pupils would be absent temporarily when they had to visit the dentist at Corfe Castle, or go to Wool to attend a confirmation class. Tom Everett was always excused in September to help with the harvest, and Harry Matthews when the threshing machine arrived. This was on the understanding that both boys returned to school once the harvest was gathered in or if the weather was too wet for any work to be done.

The teachers were conscientious and this was reflected in the reports of the Diocesan Inspector. One, signed by E.J. Tadman and read out to us by a beaming Miss Woodman, was particularly complimentary:

The teaching is thorough and the children answer brightly and thoughtfully. The school is in excellent order. The results on the whole are in advance of last year's. The quiet, reverent tone is very pleasing…

When His Majesty's Inspector came to inspect the school the best thing about his visit was that after he had gone we children were given the remainder of the day off as a half-holiday. We were all taken down to the seashore at Worbarrow in a horse-drawn waggon and the Sunday School children and members of the choir came to join us and we all had tea.

We always looked forward to Empire Day – 24 May – when in the morning we had a special lesson on our responsibilities to our country and were reminded that we were citizens of a glorious Empire which stretched right around the world. The Union flag was raised on the flagstaff on the grassy knoll outside our cottage but Miss Woodman said it might have to be moved because the cows would keep knocking it over! In the afternoon we had another half-holiday.

Helen and Bessie at Laundry Cottage.
Photo: Helen Taylor

A favourite treat was when we were invited to an afternoon tea party at Tyneham House. If the weather was fine, parties were held out in the garden under the shade of the trees. There were races along the terrace wall and we scrambled for ginger nuts and sugar-plums. Afterwards Mr W. H. Bond always gave each child a present such as a doll for the girls and a wooden train for the boys.

As children we did not usually play in the woods but Good Friday was always a special day. After Sunday School, escorted by the Misses Bond, we were invited to go to the woods near Tyneham House to pick primroses and bluebells with which we decorated the church. We would tie them up into bunches with lengths of wool and fill our wicker baskets. Afterwards, Mrs Bond gave everyone a penny and a hot cross bun. Tyneham was the only village in the area to be given the remainder of that day as a holiday, when the menfolk would go home to their gardens and observe the time-honoured custom of planting out, or 'setting', their potato crops.

My job on a Saturday was to sweep the church steps prior to the arrival of the ladies for morning service the following day. Sometimes mother sent me off on an errand to fetch a broody hen for father who was responsible for looking after the pheasants, whose eggs had a better chance of hatching out if a broody hen could be found to sit on them. One of my favourite pastimes was going to Wareham with mother and my sister Bessie. With six breadwinners in the family – father, mother, my two brothers and my stepbrothers, William and Charlie Meech – we were soon able to afford a pony and trap.

I was always the one who had to go and fetch Polly, the pony. I enticed her with a crust but was careful only to offer her half of it because I knew her all too well. She would snatch it out of my hand and go galloping off round the field and up and under the hill. When she had tired herself out and returned for the other half, that is when I grabbed hold of her! Polly's harness had a little bell – we called it a 'rumbler' – which warned people of our approach. In that way collisions could be avoided in the narrow lanes. Once people got to know us they could tell who it was by the sound before we even appeared. We took it slowly up to the top of Grange Hill, and then Polly trotted all the way down.

Our first stop in Wareham was at Dickers, the pork butchers in West Street. Here mother gave her order and the shopkeeper wrapped her groceries up for her in a neat parcel. 'Let me get aboard before you load

Emily Taylor, daughters Helen and Bessie, and pony, 'Polly'. Photo: Helen Taylor

up', mother would say to the errand boy, 'or Polly will go on home without me'! We always stopped at the World Stores to buy Polly a packet of sweets and the pony would nuzzle into my mother's pocket to get at them. When we reached the foot of Grange Hill, Polly would stop of her own accord and refuse to budge another inch, as if to say, 'If you think I'm going to pull all of you up – and all the shopping – then you've got another think coming'. So we had no choice but to get out and walk.

Everyone kept chickens and we had a pig which was kept in a sty at the back of the cottage under the trees. Pigs dislike too much sun as they have little hair and can easily get sunburned. We also had a parrot which one of the neighbours gave to us. We fed it on sunflower seeds, a few of which my father would plant at either end of his row of runner beans. When the big yellow flowers come out they attracted the bees. The bees would then pollinate the bean flowers and we would get a bigger crop. So there was method in father's madness!

A SHEPHERD AND HIS SHEEP

At the southern end of The Row lived Shepherd Lucas and his wife and their sheepdog, Sam. When he was up on the hills tending his flock, the shepherd must truly have felt that he was master of all he surveyed. To the south of the Tyneham Valley lay the jagged edge of Gad Cliff and higher still the lofty Tyneham Cap. To the north was the long range which included Grange Hill and Whiteway Hill which from there were views of the white cliffs of Arish Mell and of the Mupe rocks stretching into the sea. On the horizon, was the long and squat Island of Portland.

Every inch of every hill and field Shepherd Lucas had walked in his time – the Great Mead, the Glebe Mead, the West Eweleaze – 'leaze' being the Dorset word for pasture. Seven hundred sheep there were, up on those hills, mostly of the Dorset Horn variety but also some Shropshires which had been introduced by the Reverend Nathaniel Bond. Each sheep had a bell around its neck. An intermittent tinkle meant that all was well and a loud jangling noise told the shepherd that the sheep were agitated and on the move. Then it was his job to find the reason why; was it a fox lurking in the bracken ready to tear them apart given half a chance, or a greater black-backed gull hovering and ready to peck out their eyes and scavenge their flesh?

In the spring, when it was lambing time, we hardly saw the shepherd. He would be busy, sitting up all night if necessary to make sure the births went smoothly and that the newborn lambs took to their mothers. And when he did snatch some sleep in the back of his little covered waggon on wheels which could be pulled from place to place by a pony, he had first to make sure that his woolly charges were safe and sound in their hurdle pens. Shepherd Lucas was a man of few words. Whistle, yes, he could whistle all right, and with a variety of intonations he could control his dog, Sam, with absolute precision. However, in summertime he would boast that he would change places with no man, and that Tyneham was a place as near to heaven as it was possible to get on this earth. But in the winter, when the gales blew and snow lay on the ground and he was 'shrammed' with cold – 'shrammed' is one of our Dorset words – then it was a different story.

The flock would be brought down into the village for shearing in June. This was done in the barn by a band of travelling professionals. It was a skilled task to cut the fleece off with hand shears and avoid nicking the

The view from Tyneham Cap.

sheep – the 'gert lummocks' took fright for the flimsiest reason, which could make the shearer's life very difficult.

Shepherd Lucas told me about the time when great sheep fairs were held up on Woodbury Hill ten miles to the north above Bere Regis. These fairs were among the biggest in the South of England. There were fortune-tellers, horse-traders, swings and helter-skelters, steam-driven roundabouts and, of course, the refreshment tent. Here tea, coffee and plum pudding could be bought, or 'furmety' – wheat boiled with eggs and spices and laced with rum for those with a head for it. Peep-shows depicted such scenes as *Dick Turpin's Ride to York* and *The Death of Black Beauty*. As many as 10,000 sheep might change hands and the auctioneer would have to shout to be heard above their bleatings as he moved between the hurdle-pens clearing each one in turn.

5
THE CHURCH AND CHAPEL

Everyone in Tyneham was extremely fond of the little medieval Church of St Mary the Virgin, the first recorded rector of which, according to the plaque on the wall, was Thomas de Kingston who resigned on 1 February 1303 and was succeeded the following year by William de Cane. In the eighteen and nineteenth centuries, members of the Bond family were the rectors here for 147 successive years, beginning with Denis Bond who held the living for fifty-three years from 1742. He was followed by William Bond for fifty-seven years and finally Nathaniel Bond who, during his thirty-seven years as rector, did not live at Tyneham House, but instead on the other side of the hill at Grange.

At the harvest festival the church was always a sight to behold, not least because of the beautiful flowers, fruit and vegetables sent down from the gardens of Tyneham House. We children made brightly coloured wreaths and gathered posies of flowers to decorate the font and

The Church of St Mary the Virgin, Tyneham. Photo: Crown copyright

window sills, under the supervision of Miss Truell, the curate's daughter. The rectory servants were responsible for the adornment of the pulpit and lectern. There was always speculation as to which of us children would carry off the prize for Good Attendance and the prize for Good Answering in the Bible and Prayer Book. At Christmas time it was the same story. The best gold-embossed altar cloth was brought into use and the brass eagle on the lectern was polished until its sparkle rivalled that of the golden candelabras and the gleaming altar cross and the candlesticks.

The south transept of the church was built in 1840 to house new pews for the Bond household. The old Tyneham House pews were then made available to the congregation but the villagers of the day were not impressed and referred to the old pews as the cow stalls, a phrase which persists to this day, but is not repeated in the Bonds' hearing!

The church has a stained-glass window to the memory of Algernon Bond, the eldest son of Mr and Mrs W.H. Bond who were to be my employers from 1916. He and his brother Ralph were at Eton together. As a boy, 'Algy', as he was known, would sit for hours in the library study-ing the atlas of the world. Those were the days when a quarter of the earth's surface was coloured red, being part of the British Empire. However Algy was soon to learn that it was one thing to gaze at a map and quite another to travel to some far-flung corner of the world and learn what it costs to sustain the Empire in terms of endeavour and human life. After Eton he joined the Army and went to South Africa to fight in the Boer War as a lieutenant in the Rifle Brigade. He was severely wounded at the siege of Ladysmith and admitted to the hospital there. Although this hospital lay outside the town's perimeter fence the Boers to their credit allowed its work to continue and permitted it to be resupplied by the defenders.

When Mr W.H. Bond learned of his son's predicament he travelled to South Africa himself and, armed with whisky and provisions, hired an ox cart and two natives and joined the column of the Commander-in-Chief, General Sir Redvers Buller. When, after almost four months the siege of Ladysmith was lifted, Mr Bond was one of the first to enter the town and hasten to his son's bedside. That was in February 1900.

In thanksgiving for Algy's safe return, his parents had a new pipe organ installed in the church. This replaced the harmonium which had in turn replaced a barrel organ, which was similar to the one in nearby Steeple church but smaller, having only two barrels instead of three.

Algy, Margot, and Ralph Bond, before Algy sailed for the South African war. Photo: Mark Bond

Mrs Frend, the rector's wife, with her niece. Photo: Crown copyright

Each barrel had eight sets of staples which, as it rotated, opened the valves to let air into the pipes, with the result that 16 tunes could be played on this instrument. The wooden case of Tyneham's old barrel organ was removed to Steeple church to be used as a wardrobe for its vestry.

Algy, having escaped with his life from one drama and given himself time to convalesce, set out for India where he caught cerebral malaria which proved to be fatal.

By tradition, the rectors of Tyneham have, over the years, been responsible for taking the services at the chapel of ease at nearby Grange. The chapel was built by the Reverend Denis Bond in the early-eighteenth century.

In 1721, when the Reverend Bernard Toupe was rector, the parish of Tyneham, all 3000 acres of it, was united with that of Steeple by Act of Parliament. Since then, technically-speaking we are designated the parish of Tyneham-cum-Steeple.

The rectory, which was built in 1876, was a very grand house to the west of the church. When Canon Christopher Wordsworth became the rector in 1889 he made the mistake of felling the fir trees on the western side to improve the view.

This was undeniably a fine one, with Baltington Farm in the middle distance, the sea beyond, and the crinkled silhouette of Flowers Barrow on the skyline. However, he had failed to realise that the trees had been deliberately planted to provide a windbreak. As a result of his action the house shook in the gales, terrifying his wife and their nine children.

The Reverend Edwin George Clifford Frend, BA, Rector of Tyneham from 1933.
Photo: Kathleen Barnes

6
LIVING BY THE SEA

Mother's dream of living by the sea had become reality. To reach it we had to walk about half a mile down the path alongside the Gwyle Stream, 'gwyle' meaning a wooded glen with a stream running through it, to Worbarrow Bay with its string of fishermen's cottages dotted along the shoreline. In the summer time there was much excitement when the dark shadows of the mackerel shoals were first sighted out in the bay. When the lookout saw a shoal the cry went up, 'Get the boats. Get the nets,' and immediately, in anticipation of a good catch, a telegram was sent from the coastguard station to Wareham to alert the dealers – the Wellsteads being the main ones – to bring their carts.

A fishing boat would position itself to seaward and as the shoal neared the shore the whole sea appeared to boil as the fish thrashed about in the water. The men would rush in with their nets and haul the mackerel ashore, box them up and load the boxes into the carts. On the way back through the village one of the Wellsteads would stand on the grassy mound known as the Knapp and call at the top of his voice, 'Mack-a-low, Mack-a-low.' All the housewives, my mother included, would come rushing out with their plates and purses to buy half a dozen mackerel as a treat for our tea. Sometimes the catch would run into several thousands of fish and the smaller dealers, who could not afford to buy a cart, would have to carry their load back to Wareham on their backs. Whiting and mullet were also plentiful.

Henry Miller had been a fisherman at Worbarrow all his life. He lived at Hill Cottage at the lower end of the Gwyle Stream, with his wife, Louisa. The cottage was at the end of a 'drong', a local dialect word for a narrow lane, and lay in the lee of a conical hill known as the Tout which projected into the sea.

You could tell which Dorset village a fisherman came from by the distinctive pattern on his jersey. The Worbarrow men had three strips of ribbing on the chest, one horizontal and two vertical, with the middle filled in with little triangles to represent the waves. Although the people of Worbarrow went to church at Tyneham and collected their post from its Post Office, they were very much a self-contained community.

41

Worbarrow Bay, 1908: hauling in the catch! Photo: Joan Brachi

Worbarrow Bay and 'Tout' (conical hill). Photo: Helen Taylor

Once I overheard a conversation between Henry Miller and Mr W.H. Bond about the smuggling that used to go on at Brandy Bay, which lies at the foot of the 400ft high Gad Cliff. It was very dangerous terrain and the beach there could only be reached at low tide by a special pathway created for the purpose. The brandy was brought over by lugger in the dead of night from France. It was then stored in a cave and when the time was right, moved into Tyneham Wood where there was another cave which was well concealed, being overgrown with brambles – or 'brimbles' as we called them.

The coastguards could, and often did, create difficulties for the fishermen who depended on wood they collected from wrecks brought up on the shore to keep them warm in winter. When the Millers were drafted in to be 'extrymen' to assist the coastguards in stamping out the smuggling the Millers thought it a huge joke because, unbeknown to the coastguards, they were all part of it! The two men chuckled as they recounted the tale. It was common knowledge that the fishermen had always been deeply involved in the smuggling, and that to avoid the possibility of their storehouse in Tyneham Wood being discovered it was

Mr W. H. Bond and Henry Miller, discussing times past. Photo: Crown copyright

43

Jack Miller, Charlie Miller and Tarry Samways, fishermen of Worbarrow.
Photo: Joan Brachi

A well-earned rest! Photo: Joan Brachi

rumoured that they would slip the Reverend John Bond, the incumbent of Tyneham, a keg or two of brandy to keep him sweet. I noticed that Henry Miller, when he spoke, used the past tense, as if the smuggling was a thing of the past. However I had my own reasons for believing that this was not the case.

One day I was down at the seashore at Worbarrow when a man came into view – a stranger riding a big white horse. I guessed at once that he was a 'surveying man', one who worked for the Customs and Excise, and I was extremely frightened. He stopped, looked around for a moment and muttered disappointedly to himself, 'There's nothing here', then he went on his way. When he had gone I saw the elderly mother of one of the fishermen stand up from the bench on which she had been sitting to reveal beneath her long voluminous skirt two wooden kegs which I assumed contained smuggled brandy. The risks some mothers take for their children.

The coastguard station was in the lee of the conical hill called Worbarrow Tout, with views of Worbarrow Bay on the one side and Brandy Bay on the other. The building was black in colour, having been painted with tar to keep the weather out as it was exposed to the full force of the gales. Beside it was a stone-built Watch House which the officers could use as a lookout when on duty.

The coastguards' boat also served as a lifeboat. It had its own boathouse and slipway down to the water's edge. The lifeboatmen were equipped with cork life-jackets, but had no lifelines or the modern rocket apparatus which they had at nearby Swanage. There was another hut and a flagstaff on top of the Tout, with railings and white marker-stones leading up to it so the pathway could be seen in the dark. Similar stones were placed at intervals all along the half-mile cliff path to Kimmeridge Bay to minimise the danger of a patrolman falling over the steep cliffs. There was a signal cannon by the coastguard station and another on top of the Tout to be fired in case of emergency.

I once climbed all the way to the top of Gad Cliff with my classmates from school and the views were breathtaking. Bindon Hill, where the Norman conquerors once built an abbey, and the Isle of Portland lay to the west. To the east was the rocky outcrop called Broad Bench; the Kimmeridge Ledges which reached out into the sea like black fingers; and the promontory of St Aldhelm's Head.

Summer 1898: coastguards taking villagers on trip around the bay.
Photo: Crown copyright

Sometimes the coastguards would take people out on trips around the bay. The exercise of rowing kept them fit and healthy.

Every Friday Mr Weeks, the Coastguard Officer, would come to the school and drill us in the school yard, where we would march up and down and exercise with dumb-bells. He told us about a tragedy that occurred in 1865 when five coastguards from Worbarrow were drowned in a southerly gale when returning from Weymouth in their boat which was laden with stores. And of a strange occurrence back in 1883 when, on Christmas Eve, the Great Western Railway Company's paddle-steamer *South of Ireland* ran aground in thick fog on a rocky ledge running out to sea 200 yards east of Worbarrow Tout, below the Wagon Rock. The crew had apparently mistaken their bearings and thought they were approaching Weymouth Bay. The ship struck with such force that she went partly over and her bow became wedged in a cleft in the rock. Then she broke in two. The coastguards rendered assistance and with the help of a tug and two barges which arrived on the scene from Weymouth, all the passengers and crew were rescued.

John Weeks, coastguard officer of Worbarrow, with his men.
Photo: Crown copyright

Steamers, also from Weymouth, were able to salvage the ship's cargo of eggs, wine and drapery but the weather changed and she was ground to pieces and declared a total wreck. Her captain was later found to be responsible for the accident and dismissed by the company.

A NEW HOUSE ON THE CLIFFS

It was most unusual for the Bonds to allow any new building on their land but in 1911 a large house called Sheepleaze appeared on the cliffs to the west of the Worbarrow Tout. It had been built for the Draper family who intended to use it in the summer holidays. There were three Draper children, Christopher, known as 'Christo', his older brother Philip and their sister Mary. Their mother was called Grace. Warwick, their father, was rarely there as he was a busy barrister in London.

It was not considered proper for working people such as ourselves to associate with the upper classes but Christo was so full of life and energy, always darting hither and thither, that everybody, including me, got to know him. While Mrs Draper occupied herself in the house, the children were given little jobs to do. Christo's job was to visit Mrs Harriet Miller – wife of Charlie, another Miller fisherman, who also kept chickens – and fetch the eggs.

Mrs Draper was immensely kind to the fishermen and in the winter she bought in firewood for them. In return she was kept well supplied with fish.

When the Drapers had friends to stay they put them up in the long thatched building in the garden of Sheepleaze. They included stage and screen personalities from their London social circle and on one holiday they were joined at Worbarrow by the American film star, Mary Pickford.

The Millers' cottage, Fern Hollow, was set back a little way from the shore on the west side of the Gwyle. Harriet Miller, at one time a monitor at the village school, was a member of the church choir for forty years.

Charlie, like all the Millers, was a fisherman but the couple supplemented their income by selling chocolates, postcards and sweets to visitors. They were also great friends of the Drapers and would collect them from Dorchester when they came down from London on the train for the summer holidays. As for all the bits and bobs they brought with them, why, Charlie's waggon was overloaded with them all!

'Sheepleaze', Worbarrow, built 1910. Photo: Meg Ritchie

Christo Draper's father taking him and his brother for a ride.
Photo: Meg Ritchie

Mary Pickford (seated left) and friends at Worbarrow Bay, September, 1921.
Photo: Joan Brachi

Jack Miller and his wife Alice, nicknamed 'Miggie', lived at Rose Cottage away up on the hill on the west side of Worbarrow Bay. They met and fell in love when Jack was working in Swanage, driving an omnibus between the station and the Victoria Hotel where Rose was the hotel cook. Her full name was Alice Rose White, hence the name Rose Cottage.

Jack and Miggie, like the rest of the Millers, got on very well with the villagers and often gave them the undersized crabs and lobsters which would otherwise have been thrown back into the sea. And if anyone called at Rose Cottage there was always a refreshing glass of home-brewed beer for them which Jack would draw from a barrel which he kept in the woodshed. For a visitor, a fresh dressed crab from him would cost sixpence, and a hot lobster sandwich, ninepence.

The Millers were often to be seen making their crab and lobster pots. They wove them from withies – the stems of willow which were to be found growing in one or other of the dozen or more withy beds down

Harriet and Charlie Miller. Photo: Crown copyright

Jack and Miggie Miller at Rose Cottage. Photo: Helen Taylor

Granny Rose Miller's ninetieth birthday at Sea Cottage, with Reverend Homan.
Photo: Helen Taylor

by the Gwyle Stream and were cultivated specially for the purpose.

The Millers used to boast that their catches were consistently bigger than those of any of their neighbours, including the redoubtable fishermen of Swanage. One day Jack confided to me how this was achieved. 'We use line maps, see,' he said, and he showed me one he had made.

When the fishermen were out at sea and found themselves over a 'hot spot' where the fish were plentiful they 'took a line' or bearing from various landmarks – a particular tree, boulder, building and so forth – and drew a map of the location. With the aid of this map they could return to precisely the same place at other times.

Miggie's mother was called Granny Rose. She enjoyed a tipple now and then and her favourite newspaper was the *News of the World*. On her ninetieth birthday a party was arranged for her. Everyone was invited including the rector, the Reverend Claude Homan.

Having had a few too many drinks and being somewhat the worse for wear Granny Rose temporarily forgot that the rector was present and was heard to cry out, 'When I do die, don't let me be buried in Tyneham churchyard, else I shall come back and haunt you all!'

7

VILLAGE LIFE

The Post Office was in the line of terraced houses called The Row. Prior to 1881 all the cottages had thatched roofs but the thatch was then replaced by stone. Originally the building had been a bakery, run by Mrs Mores whose son was the baker. In those days bread was delivered around the village and to outlying farms by donkey cart, but when the Mores family moved away no more baking was done so the bread had to be imported from Hibbs, the bakers at Corfe Castle. It then became a general stores, run by a widow, Mrs Pitman. When in 1911 she married Worbarrow fishermen, Joseph Miller, Mrs Pitman retired and was succeeded by Mrs Barnes who moved in with her husband and their daughter, Phyllis. It was then that the general stores became a Post Office as well. It was hardly big enough, what with parcels arriving and waiting to be collected, and bags of flour and soda having to be stacked up on the floor and all the provisions Mrs Barnes was required to stock. These included sweets such as humbugs, liquorice and aniseed balls in tall glass jars at one old penny a bag; biscuits, wool, cottons, needles and thimbles; boot blacking, stationery and candles – for there was no electricity at Tyneham. Cigarettes were twopence halfpenny for ten, and butter a shilling a pound.

Business was brisk indeed, but I wondered whether we should soon not be able to get into the shop for clutter. A telephone had been installed in the kitchen in Mrs Pitman's time but it was not for general use. The only other place in the vicinity which had a telephone (even Tyneham House did not have one) was the coastguard station at Worbarrow Bay. Poor Mrs Barnes; whenever the telephone rang she had to drop whatever she was doing, go and answer it and then send her girl assistant running off to whoever it might be with the message.

People used to joke that Mrs Pitman in her time did not require a messenger, because her voice was so loud that people in the shop and halfway down The Street could hear every word she said. The news would be all round the village in no time, often long before the recipient got to hear about it! Nor, in Mrs Barnes's time, was the telephone for general use but she did send out telegrams, at a cost of sixpence for a dozen words and an extra halfpenny per word after that.

Mrs Barnes, the postmistress with her husband and daughter, Phyllis, outside the Post Office, 1911. Photo: Helen Taylor

GEORGE AND HIS SMOCK

One of the great characters of the village was George Richards who lived in a dilapidated cottage on the north side of the village near the Lulworth road. All his life he had been a farm labourer and it is as a very old man that I remember him. He was the last person in Tyneham to wear a smock, apart from us schoolgirls who still wore them over our dresses. Smocks were made of home-grown flax, a tough material which would stand any amount of wear and tear and keep the wearer dry in all weathers. The top part around the chest was gathered up and then embroidered with a pattern. You could tell a person's trade by his smock. A shepherd's smock might depict crooks and hurdles, whereas a carter might have whips and wheels. George's smock, if I remember rightly, had flowers and leaves – why I do not know, unless of course it came to him secondhand. If you were well off you had one smock for work and another for Sunday best.

The Bond family had a high regard for my father and appointed him parish clerk and sexton. This meant that he was responsible for lighting the church, keeping the 'tortoise' stove burning, and ringing the bells for services. It was by no means uncommon on a Sunday for father, as he was on his way from Laundry Cottage to the church to perform his bell-ringing duties, to see George Richards out working in the fields. He would then send me to go and speak to him.

'George,' I would say, raising my voice as he was a trifle deaf, 'it's Sunday.' Whereupon he would stop what he was doing and scratch his head. I repeated the words, louder this time, 'Yes, George, it's Sunday.'

'Oh well, go on w'home, s'pose,' he would reply 'I'm glad you told me, 'cos I don't know what day of the week it is, never do.'

However, all the other days of the week George, who had risen at the crack of dawn, was to be seen out in the fields hoeing the turnips and swedes. When the cattle had eaten the tops off the turnips he would grub up the roots with a hooked tool called a 'hacker' so they could eat the bottom half and nothing would be wasted.

'I s'pose by rights I should have packed it all in years ago,' he would say, 'but the truth is I've got into such a way of it that I don't think I could even if I wanted to. And if I did I should only have half a crown parish pay to live on, and what's the good of that with a small loaf being tuppence and butter a shilling a pound. And they say a pair of weekday boots has now gone up to four and eleven pence'.

George Richards, farm labourer with sister Mrs Manktelow.
Photo: Helen Taylor

Charlie Meech, 'Odd Man' at Tyneham House. Photo: Helen Taylor

Father said that if George were to get really desperate he would appeal to Mr Bond on his behalf, as there are several old and infirm folks on the estate who were looked after and housed for only a nominal rental. Help was at hand, however, in the shape of George's widowed sister Mrs Manktelow, who came to Tyneham to look after him and keep him company.

My stepbrother, Charlie, was the bailiff's horseman at Tyneham Farm as well as the 'odd man' at Tyneham House. He knew everything there was to know about horses, and although he loved them he regarded them as unpredictable creatures. His own father, my mother Emily's husband by her first marriage, had been killed by a horse when it was being taken to be shod down at Charminster near Dorchester. A steam traction engine came along and frightened the horse, which reared up and fell on top of him.

Charlie was universally popular, had a ready smile and an infectious laugh and was always up to any challenge. Most of his work was done using the 'putt', an open, two-wheeled cart drawn by a single carthorse. It was used for general ferrying about and was large enough to carry a ton of dung, when this required for muck-spreading. Afterwards he was sure to give it a thorough clean before using it to deliver and collect the laundry to and from Tyneham House and the rectory. Charlie was also responsible for collecting everybody's letters and taking them to the Post Office.

My two brothers, Arthur and Bert, also worked at Tyneham Farm with the five Tizzard brothers, who lived in one half of Gate Cottage to the south of the village by the Gwyle Stream. Stepbrother William Meech worked as gamekeeper on the Tyneham Estate.

Tyneham was a mixed farm with both livestock and arable crops and all the fields had names often indicating what purpose they were used for. For example Lower Horse Close, Rook Grove and Higher Westfield were for crops whereas Lower Cowleaze was pasture.

None of the farms round about were large enough to be able to afford a bull of their own so at the appropriate time a travelling bull was hired and taken round the whole area. Quite a celebrity, he was! Of the Tizzard brothers, Alfred and Frank were labourers, William and George were carters and the youngest, Charlie, was the carters' boy. The horses all had names – Merry, Duke, Captain and Violet.

Farm work was hard because as the seasons changed there were endless jobs to do – ploughing, sowing, weeding, harvesting, building the haystacks, layering hedges, clearing out ditches or working at the

Working in the fields (prior to Great War): standing, the Tizzards, including Frank and Alfred; seated, left to right, my brother Bert Taylor, Fred Lucas, Frank Gould, my stepbrother Charlie Meech (with dog, 'Daniel'), and Shepherd Lucas.
Photo: Helen Taylor

sawpit making the wooden bars for the gates. The roads were no more than unfenced gravel tracks. They ran through the fields, and there were gates which we called 'barways', across them to stop the animals wandering into the next field. These gates were made by setting two tall stone posts into the ground on either side of the road and then cutting planks to slide down into grooves cut into the sides of them.

THE 1914–18 WAR

One day we all filed into school in the usual way as Miss Woodman sat at her small desk by the front door ticking our names off on the register. We could see from her face that there was something wrong. She then said, 'I have an announcement to make. I am sorry to have to tell you, children, that we are now at war with Germany'.

It was 4 August 1914. I was aged twelve and would attend school for a further two years. The infants in what was called Standard One looked at one another blankly. Willie Mintern, son of smallholder Tom; William Lucas, the shepherd's son; Louisa 'Louie' Longman, daughter of the farmer at Baltington Farm and all the others. They were too young to understand what it meant. I was then in Standard Six

One of the things both boys and girls enjoyed doing at school, was making their own clothes. The school provided the material and when we had finished an item our parents were asked to pay for it. As the war dragged on we found ourselves making lots of extra clothes for the Belgian refugees who had come to England, their country having been invaded by the enemy. We also raised money for the soldiers and sailors who had been blinded in the war, and brought toys to school to send to the little invalids at the London Hospital. I was persuaded to part with a spinning top given to me for Christmas for this reason.

The war devastated our parish of Tyneham-cum-Steeple. My stepbrother, William George Meech, lost his life in the conflict, and so did my brothers, Arthur and Bert. Arthur, who had served in Palestine and was fluent in Arabic, was buried with a headstone on the slopes of the Mount of Olives, a range of hills to the east of Jerusalem. Father took the news terribly badly and spent more and more time alone in the woods. It was as if he feared to come home. Harry and John Holland of Baltington Farm were also killed, as were Charles Job Cleall and Henry George Balson.

On the north side of the hill it was a similar story. Laurence Burt, Frank Gould and Stephen Lillington all died for their country. So did Henry Ford who lived between Steeple and Church Knowle. Henry served with the Canadian forces. His father was a gamekeeper. Bernard Chilcott of Steeple and George Cooper of West Creech also perished. They were both from farming families. On the war memorial plaque, which was subsequently placed in Tyneham church, were the words:

All men must die. It is only given to a few to die for their country.

What strange sentiments to choose, I thought, when so many millions gave their lives in that terrible war. Another cause of sadness was the death of my mother. It was in 1917 and she was only fifty-two. I think she was simply worn out with work, worry, and grief for her lost children.

Just when it seemed the war would drag on for ever peace was declared and an Armistice signed. It was November 1918 and I was sixteen years old. No one felt like dancing in the streets or having parties – the parish had lost too much for that. The occasion was marked by a simple ceremony at the flagstaff and the singing of the National Anthem. The schoolchildren were told by Miss Woodman that they may give a cheer to show their thankfulness.

The horror and futility of war was brought home to me when Virtue Gould's husband, Tom, returned from the Army. Tom had started off as under-gardener at Tyneham House and rose to be head gardener when his predecessor, Mr Curtis, retired. Before the war Tom had served for a time with the Dorset Regiment at Chitral on the North West Frontier of India. He returned to the colours at the outbreak of hostilities in 1914 and served all through the four long years. On his return he was gaunt and thin and I thought he had aged terribly. He never spoke about what he had seen and suffered in France and Belgium. All we knew was that because of his fine sense of direction he had been employed to guide parties of soldiers to and from the firing line. His war experiences left Tom prone to tremors from the effects of shells, and to shortness of breath from the poison gas which had entered his lungs.

Slowly but surely with good food, good air and the company of his family and friends to revive him, Tom regained his health and strength and his period of service as a gardener at Tyneham House totalled more than forty years.

8

WORKING AT
TYNEHAM HOUSE

I left school in 1916, when the war had been in progress for two years.
My sister, Bessie, had already left to help mother with the laundry. It
was with some trepidation that I took the path from Laundry Cottage,
past the farm and Museum Cottage, to Tyneham House where I had
been appointed to the position of seamstress to work under the supervision of Miss Hurworth, who had served generations of Bonds.

The three-storied gabled building with its immaculate lawns and
exotic plants growing in tubs along the front terrace, looked simply
magnificent. I went round to the side door where Miss Hurworth met

*Tyneham House, built in Elizabethan times and home to the Bond family since
1683.* Photo: Mark Bond

me. I soon learned that she was a most meticulous person. Every single little pleat and tuck that you did for her had to be done properly. In fact, so engrossed did she become in her work, that Mrs Bond had often to find some pretext to send her out into the garden for some fresh air.

Miss Hurworth, whose room was on the first floor, came from the tiny village of Gainford just north of the River Tees in County Durham. She had been appointed to the household in 1888. Tall and thin with grey hair, she wore long skirts which made a rustling sound as they swished along the ground when she walked. Instead of making clothes for the Bond children, which was how Miss Hurworth and her assistant had

Hannah Hurworth holding Cicely's son, John Yeatman, Spring 1912.
Photo: Helen Taylor

spent so much of their time in those early years, she and I now found ourselves mending sheets, turning them side-to-middle when they were becoming worn to get the maximum amount of wear from them; making and mending curtains and covers; darning; and when the need arose, running up an item or two for the children of the village. Louie Longman was delighted when we altered a little brown suit which had belonged to Miss Margot Bond, to fit her.

Miss Hurworth taught me well and soon I was given a sewing box of my own. How busy she must have been in the old days, knitting scarves, gloves and socks and making cotton dresses, capes, drawers and petti-coats for the Bond girls, even their bonnets, as well as flannel shirts, waistcoats and trousers for the boys.

I found it strange being in such a large building as Tyneham House after our little matchbox of a cottage, and it was some time before I learned to find my way around. The Elizabethan part of the house was in two parts, the east front consisting of the library, the Oak Hall where the children used to keep their toys and the drawing room on the

Interior of Old House. Crown copyright

The Chintz Dressing Room. Photo: *Country Life* magazine

ground floor with Mr and Mrs Bond's bedrooms above. Above the porch was the date of construction: 1523. Most striking was the lavishly appointed Chintz Room which was reserved for visitors, and the adjoining Chintz Dressing Room. In a separate building at the rear was the cook's room and the kitchen with more bedrooms above, one of which was occupied by Miss Hurworth.

Early in the previous century the two buildings were linked together when a pantry, storeroom and dining room were added with a gun room, more storerooms and a schoolroom and governess's room above.

The two-storey building known as the Old House was built in the fourteenth century, with three rooms on the ground floor including a Great Hall, and two further rooms on the first floor. However, it had fallen into such a poor state of repair that the ground floor had been converted into a bakery and lodging house for a dairyman and the first floor into storerooms for fruit and potatoes.

One evening, as Miss Hurworth and I were sitting sewing together in her room, she stopped what she was doing and began to read aloud to me from the *Journal* of Celia Fiennes who, between 1687 and 1701, had journeyed all over the country on horseback, sampling the waters at every conceivable watering place. Of her visit to Tyneham she said:

> *At Tinnum Lady Larence's house there is a pretty large house but very old timber built, there I eat the best lobsters and crabs being boyled in the sea water and scarce cold, very large and sweet; most of the houses in the Island [by which she meant the Island of Purbeck] are built of stone there is so many quarrys of stone, this is just by the great cliffs which are a vast height from the sea; here is plenty of provision of all sorts especially of fish.*

When I asked who Lady Larence was Miss Hurworth told me she was the wife of Sir Robert Lawrence, who was the owner of the estate in those days. Miss Hurworth turned out to be a mine of information about the house and its occupants. She told me the mullioned windows on the ground floor of the east front had been enlarged in the nineteenth century by the then owner, the Reverend William Bond. This was at the insistence of his wife, Jane, who had suffered from having lived in dimly lit rooms behind the mullioned windows of her previous home at Stockton near Warminster, and said firmly that she did not intend to do so again at Tyneham. The year 1883 was not only the 300th anniversary of the building of the east wing of the house but also marked the 200th year of its occupancy by the Bond family. To mark the occasion all the families on the estate had been given a bountiful supply of beef and plum pudding and four hundredweight of coal.

The Bonds had employed a half-German, half-Russian governess called Anna Petrovna Sokolova. The children immediately nicknamed her 'Socky' and she was the only other member of the household staff to have a first-floor room in Tyneham House. Fortunately, it was on the south side, whereas Miss Hurworth's was on the west. The two of them did not get on.

Socky's room was next to the schoolroom where she expected the children to be ready and waiting for their lessons at 9am sharp. She could speak several languages fluently and was often heard, from the lawn outside, going through her repertoire of operatic arias and accompanying herself on the piano. She placed great emphasis, as far as her young pupils were concerned, on the virtues of good manners and deportment and she was able to forgive them the occasional lapse in their written work.

Socky's room, like Miss Hurworth's, had a small coal fire but no hot water, which had to be brought up by the servants. She complained about the cold, but it had a pleasant view looking down the avenue of lime trees. She also complained to Mrs Bond about the food, which by common consent was not all that it should have been. The problem was that because of Tyneham's remoteness, it was extremely difficult to keep a cook for any length of time. There was nothing to do in the evenings by way of entertainment and the nearest public house, the Ragged Cat, was far away up on the Lulworth Road and in any case would not have been an appropriate place for a woman to visit on her own.

To Mrs Mary Bond fell the responsibility of presiding over the large household at Tyneham. The cook had an attic room above the Chintz Room with the kitchen maid, the under-housemaid and Mrs Bond's personal maid in adjacent rooms. The scullery maid had what was called the Throne Room, also on the second floor. The footman and butler were at the rear over the west wing and in the west attic room lived a married couple – a parlourman and the head housemaid-cum-ladies'maid.

As Laundry Cottage was only ten minutes walk away from Tyneham House I continued to live at home, but was sure to arrive punctually at 7am, ready to start work. To me this was no hardship; country people are used to rising early, and often I did not return home until the late hours of the evening.

The health of the community was always a great concern to Mrs Bond. If anyone fell ill a member of the household staff would be dispatched to the sufferer with bowls of nourishing soup and pudding. If the doctor was required someone would have to go on horseback 4 miles to the village of Wool, whereupon the doctor would arrive in a dog-cart wearing a long frock coat. This process might take several hours and therefore Mrs Bond always kept a plentiful supply of medicines, bandages and herbs to hand in case of emergency. She loved music. Not only did she sing, but she also played the piano, harp and organ.

When I started work at Tyneham House Ralph, the Bond's second child, was living abroad in the Sudan and pursuing a career in the Political Service. It would be many years before his family set eyes on him again, but he communicated regularly through letters.

Cicely, the third of the Bond's five children, married barrister Lewys Legg Yeatman of Hartlebury Castle, Worcester in 1910 at Tyneham church.

What an occasion the wedding was, with Tyneham church bedecked with flowers and coachman Fred Knight sitting proudly on the Bond's coach with its coat of arms and shining brasswork, and the horses coats gleaming as if they had been polished. I shall not forget it as long as I live.

The couple set up home at Stock Gaylard, near Sturminster Newton in northwest Dorset. When they visited Tyneham, Cicely would offer to help at the Sunday School which had always been a major interest of hers and her sisters. As I, too, was often co-opted to help, I learnt a great deal from her as she reminisced to the children about Tyneham and what it meant to her.

It was the Christmas times she missed most. The three sisters – herself, Lilian and Margot – would put on entertainments which they would plan for weeks or even months ahead. At first they were held in

Cicely Bond's wedding: 1910. Cicely in front row with bouquet. Her husband, Lewys Yeatman, on her left; on his left, his father, the Bishop of Worcester (who conducted the service). Photo: Mark Bond

the schoolroom, but they proved to be so popular that they were soon looking for larger premises. Farmer Walter Case Smith offered them the use of his barn, where they built a stage and erected the scenery. Soon people were coming from miles around to the 'Tyneham Theatre', and the three young women found themselves performing in front of packed houses of 150 people.

Lilian Bond, 1887, with Amos and Daniel, her Aberdeen terriers.
Photo: Mark Bond

At Christmas time, the mummers would visit the village. A group of about a dozen men would arrive some time between Christmas Day and Twelfth Night, and no sooner had the fiddler and serpent player – a serpent being a tubular instrument with several bends in it – finished their introduction than the play began. A great favourite was *Saint George and the Dragon* with characters including the Turkish Knight, the Saracen, the Fair Sabrina and, of course, Father Christmas. After the performance the mummers were rewarded with money, and beer brewed in the brewhouse by William Woadden, the Bonds' butler. Any profit made was put by towards the fund for a recreation hut for the village.

Lilian, the Bonds' fourth child, had married Herbert Ivo de Kenton Bond of nearby Grange and they lived at Weybridge in Surrey. On her visits to Tyneham, Lilian, like her sister Cicely, also helped to run the Sunday School.

Paddle-steamers used to ply between Weymouth and Lulworth and Lilian remembered when a wooden trolley was made which could be pushed out into the water at Worbarrow Bay. This meant that for the first time the steamers could bring in provisions, and it also meant that those wishing to board the boat could now do so at Worbarrow, instead of having to row to Arish Mell and then walk to Lulworth Cove.

Margot Bond was the youngest. Unlike her siblings she did not marry but remained at home and took a lively interest in village life. Miss Margot, as we called her, was always kindness itself, and I could not help

Margot Bond. Photo: Mark Bond

Paddle-steamer Victoria *in Lulworth Cove.* Photo: Crown copyright

but reflect that although she and I were from very different stations in life, we had in common the fact that we were both single women.

It was Miss Margot who obtained a recreation hut for the village. After the war the huts at Wareham in which returning soldiers of Kitchener's army had been billeted, were put up for sale and she managed to purchase one at a knock-down price and had it brought to Tyneham and put up in the grounds of the gardener's cottage. All that now was needed was a piano and again Miss Margot was fortunate. It so happened that the school had just been given a new instrument by the Dorset County Council and when the old one, which had been purchased originally with the proceeds of a garden fête at Tyneham House, was offered to her, she accepted it gratefully.

9
TYNEHAM HEAVEN

One of my great joys was to walk on a summer's evening down to Worbarrow Bay and then up the hill towards the Minterns' cottage, where smallholder Tom Mintern's cows could be seen taking advantage of the last rays of the setting sun to graze the lush green grass of Worbarrow Tout.

Tom Mintern and his wife, Sarah, had three daughters, Winnie, Beatrice and Rose, but they always longed for a son and when their dream came true and Willie arrived on the scene they were overjoyed.

Willie was in the infants at Tyneham School when I was in the seniors. Tom grazed his heifers and cows on the Tout and also in the fields behind the rectory. Twice a day he would call with his can delivering fresh milk to the villagers' doors – one pint in the morning and another in the evening. There was a small annexe at the side of his cottage where his wife made the butter. This annexe remained thatched, even though the main dwelling had long since been tiled with stone.

Tom was the only villager apart from the Miller fishermen, the Bonds and Reggie Warr, the retired schoolmaster, allowed to keep a boat. On his fishing trips he was always accompanied by his friend 'Tarry' Samways.

Tom's assistant, Jimmy Presley, considered himself to be something of a preacher and as he went around with the milk would deliver quotes from the Bible which he invariably prefaced with the words: 'The Good Lord sayeth unto thee...' Tom said he had no objection to this, just as long as it did not put his customers off.

A WEDDING IN THE SPRING

In the spring of 1920 Mr Ralph Bond returned from the Sudan to marry Evelyn, the daughter of the late Colonel Arthur Blake. The colonel had five daughters and in the summer he and his family used to visit Smedmore House, near Kimmeridge, which was the seat of the Mansel family. That was when Ralph and Evelyn met.

Coachman Fred Knight lived with his wife and four children at

Tom Mintern. Photo: Helen Taylor

William Ralph Garneys Bond ('Ralph') as bridegroom. Photo: Mark Bond

Museum Cottage to the west of Tyneham House on the edge of Rookery Wood. Driving a coach and horses could be a dangerous occupation. Fred's predecessor, Sydney Mills, had almost been killed when the dogcart he was driving overturned in the snow. As a result of that accident he lost his nerve and never drove again.

I would often see Fred's son, young Fred, helping his father by cleaning the horses' curb chains. The animal's saliva made the chains lose their shine so they had to be soaked thoroughly in water, then buried for a time in sand and finally rubbed together to regain their sparkle.

Two or three times a week Fred senior took either the coach or the dogcart to Wareham – the choice depending on whether he was collecting visitors or just goods – and every year's quarter, when the Bonds had an order with the Army & Navy Stores in London, he would go to Wareham Station to meet the train. Then the cart was loaded with such provisions as cereals, spices, tea, coffee, sauces, pickles, potted meats, sugar loaves and such household essentials as boot blacking.

The roads had a gravel surface, there being no Tarmacadam until one reached the other side of Wareham, so it was a bumpy ride and what with all the gates having to be opened and closed, and having to wait for traffic coming the other way, it could take some time. That is why Fred senior always took someone along with him, usually young Fred, to lend a hand.

It was too much for the horses to do the journey to Wareham and back in one day so they were rested overnight at the Red Lion. Then, when they did eventually return to Tyneham House, we all had to turn to and help stack everything away in the storeroom. The horses had to be cooled off, rubbed down, fed and watered and Fred confessed that by

Cicely Bond's wedding, 1910: coachman Fred Knight and his young groom ready with coach. Photo: Mark Bond

the end of the day he was quite worn out. However, there was always the consolation of a comfortable seat by the saddle-room fire to look forward to. This was kept burning constantly to keep the harnesses and tackle dry and free from mould.

A tragedy occurred which shocked the whole village when young Fred Knight's best friend, Willie Mintern, the only son of smallholder Tom Mintern, and another boy who was visiting from London, were drowned off the headland called the Point. I shall always remember the date. It was 16 June 1923. The two boys had gone out together in a flat-bottomed boat which in all honesty they should never have put to sea in, it being more suitable for river sailing, when they were caught by the current. Both boys lost their lives but it was not until several weeks later that poor Willie's body was washed up on the shore.

Willie's death left young Fred Knight feeling quite bereft, the two boys having been very much of a kind and always getting into mischief, as when they tried to ride Miss Margot Bond's donkey and young Fred was thrown off into the stinging nettles!

ANOTHER NEW HOUSE

In the early 1920s a bungalow was built near the cliff edge to the west of the Draper family's home, Sheepleaze. It was occupied by Mrs Mary Jane Wheeler who was known to everyone as 'Auntie'. One of her forebears was Elizabeth Fry, the prison reformer, and her late husband had been a cotton magnate in the Midlands.

The Wheelers had no children of their own but when some relations of theirs who lived in Bath died, they adopted their four children (who were now grown up and in their forties).

Like Topsy, The Bungalow as it came to be known, just grew and grew until finally there were eight bedrooms and a billiards room with a full-sized table. Electricity was provided by a 32-volt petrol-driven generator for which appropriate electrical appliances and light bulbs had to be specially obtained. Mrs Wheeler's adoptive family was now spread far and wide. Winifred had married a Group Captain who lectured at Cranwell, Maud had become a secretary and moved to America, Jean had married a Scot and lived in Scotland and Trevor had emigrated to South Africa.

The Bungalow. Photo: Meg Ritchie

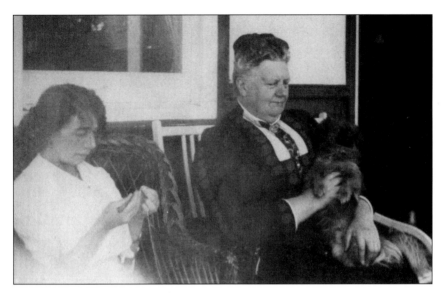

Companion and Mrs Mary Wheeler. Photo: Joan Brachi

Although she missed the children she loved the peace of Tyneham where, from her window, she could look straight out over the sea at terns diving for fish, or at dolphins who arrived as summer visitors. She was often to be seen sitting out in the garden in her wicker chair sewing and doing her embroidery. At Christmas time she would give parties for the children of the village and made sure always to provide them with a goodly supply of sweets and chocolates, home-made by Flo Davis, her parlour-maid, using special moulds.

Mrs Wheeler was distantly related to Reggie Warr, the retired school-master who lived with his wife at Gate Cottage. He had been severely wounded in the Great War and spent his days fishing from a boat he kept at Worbarrow. Neither of the Warrs enjoyed good health and Mrs Wheeler was forever sending them food parcels and nutritious bowls of warming soup.

We were always somewhat amused by the eccentric Walter Case Smith, the farmer who leased the Tyneham Farm from Mr W.H. Bond. He was known as 'Old Leatherjacket' because he invariably wore a leather waistcoat. He was forever complaining that he received scarcely more

Farmer, Walter Case Smith, at Tyneham Farm, with 20hp Austin tourer.
Photo: Crown copyright

for his produce than his predecessor, Farmer Hull, had received twenty-five years previously, and he produced some old farm ledgers from the year 1897 to prove it. They contained this entry:

> *287 couple of Rabbits sold for £29 0s 6d with cost of catching an extra £15 7s 6d. Withies 10s a cartload and 150 bundles of faggots £12.*

Farmer Smith lived in the farmhouse with his wife and a help. There was also accommodation for two lads. It was a mixed farm with arable crops and livestock. There were cow stalls, stables for the heavy horses, pigsties and a barn with granary above. On Thursdays the village street was a cacophany of sound as the bleating lambs along with calves and pigs were driven by cart to the village of Wool and from there taken by train to Dorchester to be sold in the market. Milk from the Tyneham Valley was sent by milk cart to Corfe and from there taken by train to London.

Farmer Smith kept a supply of salted fish in his dairy so when the villagers needed to buy some it saved them having to make the journey down to Worbarrow, and it brought him in a few extra coppers at the same time. His pride and joy was a new Austin 20 tourer which was the first model to be mass-produced after the 1914–18 war.

ENTER JOE DANDO

One day in 1926 a young lad knocked on the side door of Tyneham House and was answered by Rose the parlour-maid, whose full name was Alice Rose Wellman. Alice was the granddaughter of Shepherd Lucas and her father was labourer and carter at Tyneham Farm. The lad's name was Joe Dando. He had travelled all the way from Radstock in Somerset, where his father worked at the Middle Pit coal mine and his five uncles at the colliery at Norton Hill. When he was still at school Joe had worked in a ladies' haberdashery shop from 4pm to 7pm and when he left school he became a grocer's boy.

One day Joe's mother summoned him. 'The rector has been looking for you,' she said, which immediately made him think he had done something wrong. However, this was not the case. Joe's mother told him that the rector was anxious that not every boy in the village should have to face a life of unremitting toil in the coal mine, which would normally have been the case. The rule in those days, according to Joe, was that if a boy had no worthwhile job by the time he was aged fifteen then in the absence of any insurance contributions paid by an employer the boy would have no choice but to go 'down the pit'.

To avoid this happening the rector had placed an advertisement in the *Western Gazette* recommending boys for 'Gentlemen's Service', and now here was Joe, who had travelled by train to Wareham, by bus from there to Corfe, and walked the rest of the way, suitably brushed and well polished, having been summoned for interview by Mrs Mary Bond.

Joe was appointed pantry boy by Mrs Bond and was given a pair of white overalls and a cap to be worn on one side of his head. His day began at 7am when he helped prepare the breakfast and in the afternoon he took letters to be posted and collected the milk from Tyneham Farm. He always paused at the farm to look longingly at Farmer Smith's gleaming new Austin tourer!

When Joe was having his afternoon break, Rose, who was the same age as he, made the tea which was always taken in the Oak Hall. Her uniform was a white blouse, black skirt with white apron and a little half-round cap worn at the front of her head. Dinner was usually over by about 9pm, after which Joe was free. In those days there was only Mr and Mrs Bond and their daughter Margot to cater for, except, of course, when other members of the family or guests came to stay.

Joe's broad Somerset accent caused no little amusement in the house-

Joe Dando and wife Rose, who were married in 1934.
Photo: Joe Dando

hold, as no doubt our Dorset accents caused amusement to him. In fact as far as he and I were concerned, it was some time before either could readily understand what the other was saying. Before Joe left Radstock the rector had told him that he had written to the Reverend Sharpe, Rector of Tyneham about Joe, who must go and see him. However, when Joe did introduce himself to the Rector he said bluntly: 'I am new here myself, so you'll have to find your own way around.'

It was during Joe Dando's time at Tyneham that a coke boiler and radiators were installed. Until then each room was heated by an open fire. Alas, our hopes of being warm and cosy were to remain unfulfilled as the system proved to be hopelessly inefficient and the quantity of coke the boiler gobbled up was nobody's business. There was no hot water in the upper part of the house. This was brought up in brass cans in the morning for shaving and in the evening for washing before dinner. There was no electricity. Instead there were thirty paraffin lamps to be lit-and maintained.

There were shooting parties, when the villagers and fishermen would arrive to beat for the pheasants, after which steak puddings were served in the brewhouse where in winter a great fire burned. On the north wall of the brewhouse were hung Mr Ralph Bond's Oxford oars – he had gone up to New College after leaving Eton, and rowed for the University.

On Christmas day we members of the household would find presents from the Bonds on our plates as the butler Mr Tassell and his wife, Miss Hurworth, myself, Rose, Joe Dando, and the other servants had our breakfast together. Joe's present was usually a pair of socks. The cook enjoyed a glass of her own 'Botanic Beer', which she made herself using crystals. Cook usually stayed in her room and only joined the other servants at meal times in the Servants' Hall.

Joe had a secret, which I guessed soon after his arrival at Tyneham House. He had fallen in love with Rose and she with him. In fact, he told me it had been love at first sight as she had opened the door to him on that very first day when they met. I was slightly older than Joe and Rose, being now twenty-four years of age, and confessed to being quite envious of the young pair. How wonderful it must be to fall in love, I thought!

There had been great rejoicing in the Bond family when in 1924 Ralph Bond had been appointed Governor of the Dongola Province of the Sudan. Now, two years later, he returned with his wife and two children to live at Broadmayne near Dorchester. When he visited his

The Tyneham Valley. Photo: Sylvia Braisby

family at Tyneham, Ralph met Joe Dando and grew to like him immensely. Joe always said that Mr Ralph treated him as if he was his own son.

Joe was in the habit of cycling to Wareham to the barber's shop to have his hair cut. One day as he was going along the dusty roadway he happened to look back in the direction of Lulworth and was surprised to see great palls of smoke rising in the distance. When he arrived in Wareham the barber said to him, 'I suppose you have heard about Lulworth Castle? It caught fire in the night.' The castle was the seat of the Weld family. The year was 1929.

As time went by Joe's love for Rose the parlour-maid, and her love for him, grew by the day, and was plain for all to see. Then suddenly came the worst day in Joe's life. He was called for interview with Mrs Bond, who told him that he would have to leave in order to advance himself in his work. There was nothing more they could teach him. Joe was desperately upset. Not only were he and Rose courting, but he had always believed that at Tyneham he would have a job for life. He had served the Bond family for three years.

It was therefore with a heavy heart that he said goodbye. Mr William

Bond wished him good luck and said he hoped that one day Joe would have a position in a leading hotel. Rose remained behind at Tyneham House and was utterly downcast. With the departure of Joe, Rose needed the support of her friends at Tyneham House of whom I was one. She found it a comfort to confide in me and keep me up to date with Joe's progress.

Joe first obtained a position at Blandford working for a Major and Mrs Holroyd of Langton House. Then when the Major died his widow was forced because of death duties to move to a smaller house. This was at the hamlet of Fritham in the New Forest, and when she moved she asked Joe to go with her. In the meantime, Rose, who found the pain of separation from Joe too much to bear, found herself a position at Lyndhurst to be nearer to him. There was much joy when finally Mrs Holroyd invited Rose to come and be her housemaid. Thus Joe and Rose were reunited, and in 1934 they married.

The couple then moved to Stock Gaylard near Sturminster Newton in the north-west of the county, to work for Mr Bond's daughter, Mrs Cicely Yeatman. Finally, they returned to work at the Manor House at Steeple, where Rose's father worked. Rose was taken on as housemaid and Joe was given the job of chef. Finally, when Joe tired of the indoor life, he got an outdoor job working on the farm at Steeple Leaze. Events had now turned almost full circle, and Joe could look down the valley towards Tyneham with fond memories of the people there who had made him so welcome when he had first arrived, and of the house where he and Rose had first met.

10
LAST YEARS OF THE SCHOOL

A schoolmistress on a motorcycle? Surely not. But that is how Winnie Bright, the new assistant teacher at Tyneham School, travelled to work from her home at Kimmeridge where her ex-RN father, was a Coastguard Officer. Winnie had taken up her appointment at the school the previous year and every day had set off to walk the 2 miles from her home. This was an arduous journey for her with the likelihood that she would either become stuck in the mud churned up by Farmer Smith's cows, or be accosted by his flock of aggressive and ill-tempered geese!

Schoolteacher Winnie Bright, with two of her pupils. Photo: Winnie Bright

Winnie's father finally took pity on her and, to save her the walk to school, took her to Mr Blake's garage at Corfe and bought her a smart red and black Raleigh motorcycle. She rode it to and fro each day down the Valley Road.

Winnie was particularly admired at Tyneham School for her singing lessons and for her piano-playing ability. Everyone much enjoyed her repertoire of military marches. However, she was not to be there for long because, having passed the Dorset Education Authority's examination, she was appointed teacher at Herston School in Swanage, which was conveniently near to her home. Here she met and married a coastguard colleague of her father's. Her departure from Tyneham was much regretted, especially by the boys who no longer had the excitement of seeing her arrive on her motorbike.

THE CAKE FAMILY

Mabel Cake and her younger sister Violet, who were born at Osmington near Weymouth, lived at West Creech Farm on the north side of the hill near the village of Povington. Their father rented the farm from John, the son of Nathaniel Bond of Grange. I got to know the girls well. They were regular attenders at the Sunday School, where I assisted Miss Margot Bond with the teaching.

At first, both sisters attended school at Grange but because Violet was unhappy she chose to come to Tyneham School instead. She would take the steep path up over Whiteway Hill, past the smallholding at Betty Corner, where she would call on the way at Povington farm for the Wrixon children.

The village children, Cakes and Wrixons included, spent many happy evenings in the Recreation Hut playing whist or watching silent films such as *Mickey Mouse*. The rector, Mr Corfield, was in charge of the projector which he worked by the turning of a handle, and farmer's daughter, Louie Longman, provided a spirited piano accompaniment.

At the fancy dress parties I usually found myself making the tea. Mabel Cake and her friend, Elsie Taylor, once went as the characters who appeared in the advertisements for Lyons Corner House. Elsie went as Nippy, the waitress in white apron and black dress, and Mabel was Bob with her head inside a big shiny shilling, bob being the slang word for a shilling in those pre-decimal days. They won first prize, which was a set of china jugs which Mr Bond presented to them. The children's nickname for Mr Bond was 'Old Flycatcher', on account of him always going around open-mouthed.

The Cake sisters' summertime treat was to walk to Worbarrow, calling in on the way back at Longman's Farm, Baltington, where Mrs Longman, Louie's mother, would give them tea and 'dripping cakes'.

Mabel Cake and friend. Photo: Mabel Cake

Kathy Wrixon, helping on family farm. Photo: Kathy Wrixon

Kathy, another regular Sunday School attender, lived at Povington Farm with her parents and her four brothers, Fred, Walter, William and Len. Kathy and Walter also made the long journey to Tyneham School, taking with them William, known as 'little Billy'.

When he was very young Billy had difficulty with his words and would open his Prayer Book, see a picture of a lamb and cry 'Poor little weep, lost its mother.'

When we took him on a Sunday School outing and he was walking through a clump of rhododendrons he was heard to say, 'What do I well wetted?'

Luckily, Kathy was able to translate. 'Well' meant 'smell' and 'wetted' meant 'scented', hence 'What do I smell [that is] scented?'

In wintertime when the gales blew and the children were 'shrammed' with cold, little Billy often had to hang on to the fence to avoid being blown away. A gale, the worst in living memory, came in the month of December 1929 and none of us would ever forget it. It blew for several days and cut great swathes through Rookery Wood, West Plantation and Great Wood, destroying many trees. Worst of all our precious Recreation Hut was lifted right off the ground and deposited in pieces in the woods. Where the piano went, nobody knew!

Everyone was desperately upset but Miss Margot Bond would not be defeated. She went straightaway to the Ideal Home Exhibition in London and bought a brand new hut for £120, together with chairs, crockery and some oil stoves with which to heat it. However this time she insisted that it be placed up in the woods near Museum Cottage as the previous situation was clearly too exposed.

SYLVIA HOUSE

Sylvia, daughter of Herbert and Jessica House, was brought up with her five siblings at Serley's Living Cottage, Povington Farm, which was also on the north side of the hill. Her father rented the farm from the Bonds of Grange.

Sylvia's first went to East Lulworth Church of England School and from there she transferred at the age of eleven to Tyneham School. When her father made the children a wooden sleigh with seats, they dragged it through the snow to the top of one of the ancient Iron Age burial mounds and took it in turns to sit on it and speed off down the hill. When a neighbour Mrs Cooper, who lived at the farm nearby, came out and joined them they persuaded her to have a go. They gave her a push and away she went, only to fall off and end up down at the bottom with a broken leg. This was the same Mrs Cooper who liked to buy herself a hat at the jumble sales which were held from time to time at the Recreation Hut.

Sylvia's family knew how to celebrate Christmas, when each child would hang up a stocking on Christmas Eve and next morning find in it an apple, some nuts or

Sylvia House, wearing medal which she won for netball when at school in Corfe. Photo: Sylvia House

perhaps a sugar mouse. The very fortunate ones might receive a wooden hoop or train, or a top with a whip to make it spin. One birthday, Sylvia's mother took her to Wareham. This meant crossing the Common and taking the 'Cat Road' from East Lulworth, so-called because there was once a public house there called the Ragged Cat. From there they caught the motor coach into town where her mother bought her a little sewing box.

Sylvia would dread her mother asking her to go on an errand to Tyneham Post Office in case Farmer Smith's cows were loose, as there were no fences and she knew that the bull was likely to be in with them. This meant pushing her bicycle all the way up to the top of Grange Hill and then free-wheeling all the way down. One day Sylvia met the herd coming the other way. She scrambled up onto the bank and hid in a bramble bush, whereupon the bull stopped, sniffed at her bicycle and then proceeded to lick it all over before going on his way. Sylvia shook for quite a time afterwards, and when she told us about it none of us were surprised. It was everyone's dread to meet the bull for they are dangerous and unpredictable creatures.

Sylvia would attend Tyneham School for one term only because it was decided that all eleven- year-olds must in future attend school in Corfe. It was too far for her to walk so Mr Sheasby ferried her to and fro in his taxi. He ran his taxi business single-handed, having begun years previously by ferrying passengers to and from the railway station at Corfe in his horse and cart.

The liveliest little boy in the whole of the parish of Tyneham-cum-Steeple was, in my opinion, Arthur Grant. His family had moved to Tyneham from Galton near Dorchester in the year 1924 and his father had succeeded my father, who had by now retired, as estate woodman at a salary of £1.10s per week.

Like all the other cottages his, which was situated alongside the Gwyle, had no electricity or running water. Sanitation was a bucket outside the back door.

Arthur always looked forward to Sundays because this was the day he pumped the church barrel organ at morning service as Mrs Bowdidge of Grange played the hymns. For his service, Arthur was rewarded with a sixpence. An enterprising boy, was young Arthur. He discovered that a good way of making extra pocket money was to volunteer to open and close gates for the increasing number of motorists who began to come from far afield to visit Worbarrow Bay. There were four gates, and

Arthur and his friends quickly realised that it paid to get up early and man the nearest gates, to spare themselves the necessity of having to travel further afield.

A penny or two was thrown from the cars as a reward, and on a good day a boy might take home as much as three or four shillings. The boys saved their money, which they put towards their annual Sunday School outings to Weymouth and Bournemouth.

A famous visitor to the area was T E Lawrence, the famous Lawrence of Arabia whose exploits everyone had heard about. Lawrence used to get very annoyed when he found that all the gates between Creech Hill and Worbarrow were kept shut, so he would charge them head-on on his motorcycle to burst them open. This made him unpopular with the farmers who one day decided to catch him out by locking them.

When Arthur Grant left school I followed his career with interest, knowing that his life would never be dull. Sure enough he joined the Merchant Navy and when he returned from Africa on leave he brought back with him a chameleon which he gave to the Bond children.

They were fascinated by its ability to change colour, and they let it roam around in the tubs of geraniums which stood in pots at the west front of Tyneham House. One day, however, it came to a sticky end when it strayed onto the lawn and was run over by the lawnmower which was a contraption operated by two gardeners, one who pushed it and the other who pulled. Poor chameleon, it was hidden too well for its own good. This was one time when its camouflage failed to work in its favour.

Mr and Mrs Ralph Bond had two children, Elizabeth and Mark, and we saw a great deal of them when their parents returned from the Sudan and came to visit Tyneham from their home in Dorchester.

Mark and Elizabeth Bond.
Photo: Mark Bond

This was usually in the school holidays when Mark was down from Eton. Elizabeth and Mark grew up all too quickly and I have an abiding memory of them both sitting up on the cart, each on a wicker basket full of laundry, as Charlie Meech made his way to Laundry Cottage from Tyneham House.

When Tyneham School was forced to close in 1932 everyone was immensely sad. Numbers, which had risen to a record sixty-eight pupils when the Coastguard Station had been operational prior to 1912, had fallen to an all-time low of thirteen. The children now had to be conveyed to Corfe by Mr Sheasby in his taxi, although there were some who were obliged to walk all the way to Lulworth to school.

Miss Hannah Hurworth died on 11 October 1933 at the age of eighty-six. She had served the Bond family devotedly for forty-five years.

A NEW TENANT AT TYNEHAM HOUSE

Mr W. H. Bond died in 1935 at the age of eighty-three and was buried in Tyneham churchyard. His widow Mary, and her daughter Margot, moved to Dorchester, and Tyneham House was let to a Doctor Sauer, a wealthy man who was believed to have substantial interests in the gold mines of South Africa. Dr Sauer's chauffeur, who drove the Rolls-Royce, was accommodated in Museum Cottage. I was still required to do sewing when the occasion demanded, but the whole atmosphere changed. The spirit seemed to have gone out of what had been a home of much jollification and liveliness. However, in 1938 Doctor Sauer's tenancy expired and Mr Ralph Bond, with his wife Evelyn and the children, came back to the house to live.

Following the death of Mr W. H. Bond a number of improvements were made to Tyneham House. Electric light was installed, and a telephone, the number of which was Kimmeridge 223. This reminded me of the time of Mr W. H. Bond's great battle with the General Post Office back in 1929 when it proposed to erect a new telephone box in the village and declared that its colour had to be red. Mr Bond argued that this would be a disgrace and an eyesore. He would prefer that the telephone box, if it were to be placed there at all, should be built of stone. A compromise was eventually reached and a concrete box was erected and painted white.

When Kathy Wrixon of Povington Farm married Cyril Barnes at

Cyril Barnes on one of the new tractors with father, Harry. Photo: Cyril Barnes

Tyneham church on 4 October 1938, no one was more delighted than I. Kathy's new husband, Cyril, and his family had moved from Somerset to Manor Farm, East Stoke near Wool, in 1930, and five years later the couple had met at a dance in Wareham. Kathy was then helping her parents at the farm. After the wedding they stayed at the farm for a short time before moving to Somerset.

The first tractors which we had ever seen arrived in the Tyneham Valley in 1937. They were Fordsons made in America, and each cost £125. On the wheels were spade lugs made of metal to provide traction, instead of rubber tyres. These had the disadvantage in bad weather of causing the tractor to dig itself into the ground. Sometimes after sitting out on the Fordson all day in the cold and wet of winter, George Braisby said he felt frozen stiff and could hardly dismount from the seat.

George Braisby's father became something of a celebrity in the valley when he bought a 1919 Willey's Overland car, also manufactured in America by the Chevrolet company. It was a grey touring model with a soft top and large shiny headlights. It had no windscreen wipers but George said that by cleaning the windscreen with a potato cut in half, this ensured that the rain ran smoothly off it.

11
ASPECTS OF WAR

Great Britain had declared war on Germany on the 3 September
1939 and since then approximately half of the entire area of
Purbeck was taken over by the Army, its land being in great demand
with the expansion of the Tank Gunnery Ranges at Lulworth.

Ralph Bond organised the local Home Guard; his wife, Evelyn, joined
the Women's Voluntary Service and ran a canteen in Wareham and a
mobile canteen to serve the isolated anti-aircraft batteries which were
situated all over the countryside. Their son, Mark, left Eton in August
1940, served for a few weeks in his father's Home Guard platoon at
Tyneham, and in September enlisted in the Rifle Brigade and was
commissioned the following year.

There was great excitement over at Povington Heath in July 1940
when an enemy aircraft was shot down. It crash-landed and its two
crewmen were taken prisoner. The only Germans I had ever seen were
three other prisoners who were delivered daily in an Army truck to help
Farmer Smith at Tyneham Farm. They seemed cheery enough fellows
and, as far as the war was concerned, I should say that by the look of
them they were glad to be out of it.

Watching those young men at work brought home to me the futility of
war. It all seemed so pointless, this tearing apart of so many people's
lives simply because of politics and greed.

Ralph Bond was an enthusiastic member of the Dorset Natural History
and Archaeological Society and the fact that there was a war on did not
deter him from continuing to organise field trips around Tyneham. He
was proud of the fact that the Great Wood, which had been so ravaged
by the gale of 1929 when many of its sycamore trees were destroyed, was
beginning to recover and once again provide a roosting place for the
owls. He was invited to give a lecture on Dorset bats to the Nature
Reserve Investigation Committee, a body which proposed that the State
should take much greater responsibility for the conservation of plants
and wildlife.

In 1942 Mr Ralph learned that his son Mark had been wounded in the
Battle of El Alamein, but that mercifully he had survived. In the same
year, the Grant family left Tyneham, Arthur to join the Merchant Navy

Ralph Bond, his daughter Elizabeth, wife Evelyn and son Mark in 1941, at east door of Tyneham House. Photo: Mark Bond

and serve on ships of the Union Castle Line carrying British troops to the Middle East and Royal Air Force pilots to Canada for training.

On 17 November 1943, as the village children were gathering up holly and mistletoe from the woods in preparation for Christmas, postman Barlow drew up to Tyneham House. By now he had graduated from a bicycle to a motorcycle and sidecar. The postman brought with him two letters for Mr Ralph Bond, one informing him that his son, Mark, was 'missing in action' in Italy, and the other that the Army proposed to take over the entire Tyneham Valley. Everyone was to be evacuated within twenty-eight days.

WARTIME WEDDINGS

When Mabel Cake of West Creech Farm, she of fancy dress fame, married Percy Taylor in 1941 at Steeple church, Great Britain had been at war with Germany for two years. Since leaving school Mabel, and her sister Violet, had helped their parents on the farm, taking it in turns to get up at half past four in the mornings to milk the cows. Percy worked for Mr John Bond of Grange as estate woodman and part-time keeper. His family lived at Rookery, a smallholding at West Creech. When he and Mabel married they moved into Orchard Cottage.

Two years later Violet followed her sister's example and married Cyril Burt of nearby Whiteway at the church of Lady St Mary, Wareham, and Sylvia House, my former Sunday School pupil of Povington Farm, married George Francis Braisby on 23 May 1943. George came from Blackmanston, Steeple. He had attended school at Kimmeridge and afterwards worked on his father's farm, which is where the newly married couple set up home. I remember their wedding so clearly. It was a glorious day and I made a daisy chain for them to break as they came out of the church and went down the steps. Little did we know then, but this was to be the last wedding ever to take place at Tyneham church.

THE EVACUATION OF THE VILLAGE

The winter of 1943 was a bitterly cold one and, having been served with the eviction order, the villagers' sense of gloom and bewilderment deepened even further when they realised that they had no idea of

Sylvia House and George Braisby on their wedding day.
Photo: George and Sylvia Braisby

where they were meant to go. It fell to Mr John Durant-Lewis, deputy clerk of the Wareham District Council, to find accommodation suitable for all the displaced people. He was assisted in his task by Mrs Evelyn Bond, who described it as 'the worst job I have ever had to do'.

Joe Dando and Rose were fortunate in that their cottage, and the farm at Steeple Leaze where Joe worked, were safe. They were within land just outside the border of the area which the Army had demarcated for its own use. Sylvia and George Braisby of Blackmanston, Steeple, were similarly fortunate. However, others were less so.

The evacuation of Tyneham House by the Bond family was of necessity so hastily performed that many of their belongings were broken or were subsequently damaged. This was partly because the heavy Royal Air Force lorries had fractured the drainage pipes, which caused the cellar in which the belongings were stored to flood. The Bonds had to use the cellar because of the lack of appropriate warehouse space and means of transportation, and many valuable items including clocks, furniture and carpets were ruined.

Some panelling from the medieval hall of Tyneham House was fortunately rescued and sent for safe keeping to the Dorchester Museum. Mr
and Mrs Bond moved to Corfe, as did I, with my sister Bessie and
stepbrother Charlie Meech. A bungalow was found for us there and for
the first time in our lives we had indoor sanitation and electricity. The
joy of such luxuries was, however, tinged with sadness at having to leave
our beloved Tyneham.

The Mintern sisters were found accommodation at Upwey near
Weymouth. There, not only were they far from home but they also
found themselves on a main road and adjacent to an hotel of ill repute.
Being devout Christians this was anathema to them, and they were
deeply disturbed and dissatisfied with such a state of affairs.

Jack Miller the fisherman and his wife Miggie were rehoused at
Langton Matravers near Swanage, and how they missed their former
home by the sea.

The *Dorset Chronicle* made for heartbreaking reading, particularly for
the poor farmers. Henry Duke & Son auctioned no less than 313 dairy
cows and bulls, 9 working horses, 71 sheep, 33 pigs, 167 poultry, 4
Fordson tractors and more than 700 lots of farm implements, and this
was from the Tyneham valley alone. People's lives, in fact a whole way
of life, disintegrated in a very short space of time.

Not only was Tyneham evacuated but also a considerable part of the
former parish of Steeple including West Creech and Povington. When
Kathy Barnes's parents were evacuated from Povington Farm, the two
younger boys, William and Leonard, were still living at home. The
Barnes were obliged to put their furniture into store and move in, first
with one of their grown-up children and then with the other, until they
could find another farm.

Mabel Taylor and her husband, Percy, of Orchard Cottage, West
Creech, were housed in a recreation hut beside an Army shooting range,
prior to moving into the cottage next door to Charlie Beauchamp the
postmaster. When Mabel went back to her home to collect her furniture
and the contents of the shed including the lawnmower, she noticed that
the fireplace had been removed and also the copper in which all the
family's washing was done. So there was vandalism and looting even in
those days.

Now it was the turn of auctioneers Thomas Ensor & Son to sell off the
livestock and farm implements of those living on the north side of the
hill. However, because it was known to the buyers that the vendors had

Bull being loaded onto cart on way to be auctioned. Photo: Crown copyright

to sell, the prices achieved were artificially low. This was another blow to befall the hapless villagers.

The list of displaced farmers made for sad reading. This included the Cakes of West Creech, the Wrixons of Povington, the Coopers of Povington and the Sampsons of East Lulworth. Poor William Wrixon, Kathy's brother, was due to celebrate his twenty-first birthday on 15 December. In truth, there was now very little for any of us to celebrate.

So the Tyneham and Steeple communities which had existed since time immemorial were now dispersed and their members, many of them elderly and frail, separated from one another and therefore denied the social intercourse and mutual emotional support which would have proved so beneficial at this time of crisis. We prayed that one day, when the war was over, we could all return to our homes and begin our lives anew.

12
THE ARMY STAYS ON

The war in Europe ended on the 8 May 1945. We thanked God for the victory and now realised why the Army had needed the land of Tyneham-cum-Steeple so desperately. It was there that the Gunnery Wing of the Royal Armoured Corps Fighting Vehicles Unit had trained the British and American tank crews for the assault on the Normandy beaches, and in particular the American Second Armoured Division with its Sherman tanks.

In that same year Mr Ralph Bond, who was living with his wife in temporary accommodation at Corfe, was appointed High Sheriff of Dorset. The following year, when his Uncle Harry died, they moved into Moigne Combe near Dorchester, with their daughter Elizabeth and son Mark, who to everyone's relief had survived the war.

At Corfe, in order to make ends meet, my sister Bessie and I took in laundry from the neighbours while we waited expectantly for permission to return to Tyneham. We also expressed, in a letter to the War Office, concern about the deteriorating condition of our cottages. However, in 1947 the Government announced that the Army was not to give up its occupancy of the parish of Tyneham-cum-Steeple after all. Instead, the War Department had decided that the area was to become part of the 7200 acre tank and gunnery range administered by the Army's School of Gunnery at Lulworth.

Mr and Mrs Bond, who came to visit us from time to time at Corfe, were dreadfully upset. Ralph felt that this decision by the Government was nothing less than a breach of honour. He believed that a promise had been given and that this promise had been quite deliberately broken. One outcome was that the villages in the Army's designated area became the only ones in Dorset to record 'population nil' on their electoral registers.

Among all these bad tidings came the good news of the marriage of the Bonds' daughter Elizabeth to Sir David Williams of Bridehead, Littlebredy, near Dorchester.

In 1949 Mr W.H. Bond's widow Mary died, but because Tyneham church was now in a derelict condition she could not be buried there beside her late husband. Instead, she was buried at the cemetery at

Dorchester. Margot, with whom she had been living, was then joined by her sister, Lilian, and Lilian's husband Ivo, who had now retired. When Ivo died some years later, Lilian and Margot moved to Poole.

Ralph Bond died in 1952 at Moigne Combe. He was seventy-two. Later that year the Tyneham Estate was subject to a compulsory purchase order, and Mark Bond was paid compensation by the Government for the wartime loss of the family's estates. However, he was now faced with having to pay death duties on his late father's estate. His mother, Evelyn, died two years later and she was buried, as her late husband Ralph had been, at Owermoigne near Dorchester.

In that same year, 1952, my own father, William, died at the age of eighty-seven. He was buried at Corfe cemetery in a peaceful place in the lee of the ruined castle.

Sadly, there was no compensation for us villagers as we did not own our homes. All we received from the Ministry of Defence was the estimated value of the crops in our gardens which amounted to between £10 and £20. In the 1950s the well-meaning Wareham Council, in an attempt to keep as many of the villagers together as possible, erected for them some pebble-dashed prefabricated houses. Ironically, the road in which they were situated was named Tyneham Close.

In 1967 some of the surviving villagers formed themselves into The 1943 Society, held candlelit vigils and sent a petition to Number 10 Downing Street. Alas, their efforts to make the Ministry of Defence change its mind about Tyneham's future were all in vain.

In 1971, my stepbrother, Charlie, died at the age of eighty-seven. He was buried in Tyneham churchyard and so, in a sense, came home.

In 1972 Mark Bond retired from the Army. He had served for two years as ADC to Field-Marshal Bernard Montgomery and seen active service in Kenya, Malaya, Cyprus and Borneo and after the war he had joined the Parachute Regiment. When he returned to civilian life he followed the family tradition of voluntary public service in Dorset.

In 1973, in response to further petitioning, Lord Nugent's Defence Lands Committee recommended that the Tank Gunnery School at Lulworth be moved to Wales. However, the Government decided that this was not feasible as it would cost £14 million.

In 1974 the Government pledged the sum of £10,000 to give the public greater access to the Tyneham Valley on those weekends when the Army was not using it for gunnery practice.

Mark Bond.

In 1976 work was begun to make the buildings of Tyneham safe, by removing their roofs and reducing the height of their walls. The village school remained intact, as did the Church of St Mary after repairs were made to its roof.

In 1977 Mark Bond was invited by the Army to plant an oak tree in the village of Tyneham to commemorate Queen Elizabeth II's Silver Jubilee.

THE CHURCH IS RESTORED

When the Government made the decision to grant the public access to the Tyneham part of the Army Ranges, Roy Cobb, once a stonemason and quarryman of Langton Matravers and latterly Range Warden Supervisor at Lulworth Camp, assisted by a band of willing helpers, began in 1975 the delicate task of restoring the church's graveyard to its former immaculate state. This entailed six months of cleaning and scrubbing, at the end of which it was possible to read the inscription on virtually every tombstone. Crosses which were broken were repaired; grave stones which were leaning over were straightened. When they witnessed the transformation, those who had relatives buried there were most gratified to see it. It was also now possible to walk from Tyneham to Flowers Barrow along a newly created footpath.

And then, thanks to the generosity of the Royal Armoured Corps Gunnery School Silver Jubilee Project, the Church of St Mary, Tyneham which had been declared redundant and deconsecrated by the Church authorities and leased to the Army for a peppercorn rent, was restored. A start was made and by 1979 some of the original windows were replaced, some pews restored, and a pair of wrought-iron gates given by the Royal Electrical and Mechanical Engineers installed to separate the nave from the chancel.

The lead which originally covered the roof of the nave had been stolen soon after the evacuation and been replaced by felt, but the Army have since replaced this with a tiled roof. Of the church's two bells, one is now stored at Steeple and the other hangs in the belfry of West Parley church, near Bournemouth. The Jacobean pulpit is on loan to Lulworth Camp's chapel.

In 1965, twenty-two years after the Bonds were forced to leave, an architect's report to the Ancient Monuments Board for England stated that the roof of the main Elizabethan part of Tyneham House had been

Steeple churchyard: tombs of the Bonds.

lost and that the fourteenth-century part had collapsed internally. The damage was entirely attributable to climatic conditions and there was no evidence that it was caused by shell fire. The cost of preventing any further deterioration was estimated to be £8000.

In the circumstances, and because the house lay within the firing range boundaries which meant access for building workers would of necessity be limited, it was decided to abandon any idea of restoration. Instead, with the agreement of the Ministry of Defence, Robert Cooke MP and Lord Southborough were granted permission to remove certain items including the Elizabethan porch, the ashlar facing stones of the front of the house, window frames, roofing tiles and the crest from the front door, to be incorporated into their own homes, Athelhampton and Bingham's Melcombe respectively. Other artefacts were removed to Cranborne Manor and the National Trust property at Fiddleford Mill, near Sturminster.

A SPECIAL SERVICE

Some of the former residents had kept their 1943 Notice of Taking of Possession order signed by Captain Miller of Southern Command, and still had them in 1979 when a special service was held for the former parishioners in Tyneham's reopened church. This was the first service to be held there since 1943.

What was described as a sentimental journey for the many of us was, in fact, heartbreaking. Many of the former residents were dead and their loved ones who were left wished they could have lived to see the beautiful church of Purbeck stone reopened and again in use. It was full to overflowing for the service, which was conducted by the Reverend Gerald Squarey, rector of Corfe Castle. Five robed clergy were present and the county was represented by Mark Bond's sister, Elizabeth, now Lady Williams of Bridehead and the first woman to be High Sheriff of Dorset.

My immediate family had of course long since departed this life, and yet as I listened to the rector's words, I felt they were all there with me in spirit.

The irony of it all was that when Mark Bond arrived he was told by the wardens in charge: 'The church is full. You cannot go in.' He told them that he had to get in somehow as he had been invited to read the lesson!

MEG RITCHIE'S MEMORIES

It was at this special service in 1979 that I was reacquainted with Meg Ritchie, the granddaughter of Warwick and Grace Draper who had built Sheepleaze up on the cliff at Worbarrow in 1910. She told me that their eldest son, Philip, had joined the Shell Oil Company when he grew up and their younger son, Christopher – we knew him as 'Christo' – was the author of a number of children's books and had spent some time in Africa living with the Zulus. Their daughter Mary, who was to be Meg's mother, married electrical engineer James Ritchie and they set up home at Chiswick Mall opposite Chiswick Eyot on the River Thames.

Meg remembered with affection the holidays she spent at Worbarrow in the 1930s. She told me of the day that Jack Miller, the fisherman, rowed her round to Brandy Bay and showed her a cave there which was only accessible by boat. The entrance was found with difficulty by lining

Meg Ritchie in her holiday wonderland!

Kimmeridge Bay (where Meg's parents purchased a holiday cottage); William Stickland striding up hill. Photo: Meg Ritchie

up two rocks, and even so there was only just enough room for the boat to enter. Inside was a raised platform which, Jack said, was always higher than the highest tide and legend had it that this was where smuggled goods were stored.

During the war, when the Army had moved in to Tyneham-cum-Steeple prior to the evacuation of the villagers, Meg's mother was down at Sea Cottage visiting Jack and Miggy Miller when she had a shock. A cat trod on a landmine which the Army had laid and the explosion was so great it blew off part of the Millers' roof!

Meg's parents had been obliged by the Army to abandon Sheepleaze in 1943, so they bought a holiday cottage at Kimmeridge.

Having an inquiring mind, Meg wondered what had become of Tyneham House and her adventurous nature led her on several occasions to come over from Kimmeridge and trespass on the forbidden Army ranges.

She told me that she always took care to walk on open land and not through the undergrowth, for fear of treading on an unexploded shell.

She found that to stand in the Oak Hall with the eyes from the numerous animal trophy heads Ralph Bond had brought back from the Sudan was an eerie experience. On one of her visits Meg disturbed some men with a van and she guessed that they were there with the intention of stealing materials from the site.

Meg embarked on a career as an actress, thanks in part to Alec Guinness, later Sir Alec, who lived in the house next-but-two from hers in London. Despite the noise she made as she roller-skated along the pavement outside his house in the early hours of the morning, the famous actor took a liking to the young lady.

He entered her for a screen test for the film *Alice in Wonderland*, which was to be made by Walt Disney, part real and part cartoon. However, as far as Meg Ritchie was concerned, Tyneham would always be her wonderland.

13
WHISPERS IN THE WIND

A strong spiritual presence hangs in the air over Tyneham and Worbarrow Bay, and nowhere is this presence more strongly felt than in the church. Its exquisite east window was designed by Martin Travers as a memorial to Mrs Grace Draper of Sheepleaze, Worbarrow. It depicts the Madonna and Child beneath a living tree where butterflies float about its branches. One, a Camberwell Beauty, rests in a fold of Mary's robe. On either side are scenes of Tyneham life, with fishermen putting out to sea in their boats and labourers toiling in the fields.

The Street and The Row with its ruined cottages, still seems to ring with echoes of the past, the voices of children chanting by rote from the schoolroom, the distinctive ring of Postman Selby's bicycle bell, the sound of light hooves as Emily's pony cart speeds past and the eager chatter of people catching up on news in the Post Office.

The village is now forever frozen in the year 1943, its sounds no more than imaginary whispers in the wind.

In sacrificing their homes, not only were the villagers saying farewell to their familiar way of life, they were also leaving behind traditions passed down from generation to generation and specific to their own community.

However, by this very sacrifice, Tyneham has been spared the pressures which many other Purbeck villages have succumbed to. Here are no shops or kiosks, no caravan or camping sites to shatter that peace which has been maintained throughout the ages. Mark Bond is adamant that even if the Army had not taken over, such despoilation would not have been allowed and he points proudly to his family's safe custodianship of the Tyneham Estate over the past 300 years.

It was heartbreaking for the Bond family to have to say goodbye to their ancestral home, which was fragmented and plundered by owners of other manor houses in the area. Yet Ralph Bond, who was a keen naturalist, would have been pleased to know that the sacrifice made has resulted in the area retaining wildlife that would otherwise have gone. Tyneham and its surroundings supports a butterfly unique to this isolated part of Dorset, called the Lulworth Skipper. Small and brown, with light edges to its wings, it is nevertheless beautiful and special in its own right.

Tyneham Church: the Grace Draper memorial window.

The resident pair of peregrine falcons, which nest up on Gad Cliff, can be seen in spring and summer as they soar high above with distinctive cries in the hope of snatching some poor misguided pigeon from the skies.

The gwyles provide cover for foxes, rabbits and small deer. In spring, shy primroses emerge and bluebells, like those Helen Taylor used to gather with her schoolfriends in days gone by to decorate the church, paint the woods in a riot of colour. Wild garlic grows freely, as does the poisonous but pretty Fly Agaric which is the toadstool most favoured in fairy stories with its umbrella shape and bright red cap with small white patches.

It is to be hoped that those who are moved to visit Tyneham will even now enjoy the peace and tranquillity which it has to offer and gain an insight into a way of life that is no more.

POSTSCRIPT FROM THE AUTHORS

The Army can in no way be blamed for its continued presence in Tyneham. The decision that it should remain there has been a purely political one, and it must be commended for attempting to open up the area as much as possible for visitors, bearing in mind the constraints of safety. Great efforts have been made by the Army to make visitors welcome, that is when the Firing Ranges are not in use. It has even placed, beside one of the stiles on the cliffs, a special dog door to provide easy access for canine companions.

The number to ring for information about when the Army ranges are open and when it is possible to visit Tyneham is 01929 404819

The parish of Tyneham-cum-Steeple: a typical cottage.
Photo: Crown copyright

BIBLIOGRAPHY

Bond, Lilian, *Tyneham, A Lost Heritage*, The Dovecote Press, 1956
Bond, Martin, *A Dorset Family*, Published privately
Hutchins, John, *The History and Antiquities of the County of Dorset 1774*
Knight, Fred, *The Rooks in the Elm Trees*, Myrmica Books, Wareham, 1994
Legg, Rodney, *Tyneham, Ghost Village*, Dorset Publishing Company, 1998
Leighton, Brian, *A Short History of Tyneham*, Printed by Media Support
  Wing, RAC Centre, Allenby Barracks, Bovington, Dorset
Lewer, David and Smale, Dennis, *Swanage Past*, Phillimore, 1994
Morris, Christopher, *Journeys of Celia Fiennes*, Cresset Press, London

Bournemouth Evening Echo
Dorset Magazine

Dorset Record Office: Tyneham National School Log Book 1914–1942
Tyneham Parish Registers, Tyneham Church Monumental Inscriptions